HOW TO
WIN
AN
ARGUMENT

SECOND EDITION

SUREFIRE STRATEGIES
FOR GETTING
YOUR POINT
ACROSS

MICHAEL A. GILBERT

MJF BOOKS
NEW YORK

Published by MJF Books
Fine Communications
Two Lincoln Square
60 West 66th Street
New York, NY 10023

How to Win An Argument
LC Control Number 00-136519
ISBN 1-56731-443-0

This edition published by arrangement with John Wiley & Sons, Inc.

Manufactured in the United States of America on acid-free paper

MJF Books and the MJF colophon are trademarks of Fine Creative Media,
Inc.

10   9   8   7   6   5   4   3   2   1

To Zack,
who's always a winner

Contents

Preface ix

Part One   The Art of Argument 1

1   What Are We Arguing About? 3
2   Why Argue So Much? 8
3   Types of Arguments 12
4   Defensive vs. Offensive Argument 15
5   Some Warnings 19
6   Super-Rule I: Never Admit Defeat 23
7   How Are Arguments Built? 29
8   The Principle of Rationality 34
9   Two More Principles 39
10 Super-Rule II: Listen! 46
11 Zen and the Art of Argument 50
12 Part One Review 54

Contents

Part Two   The Ways of Argument 57

13 What's Going On Here? 59
14 Ring Around the Argument 63
15 What Were We Talking About? 72
16 Everyone's Doin' It, Doin' It, Doin' It 82
17 Well, If He Said So 88
18 The Refuge of Scoundrels 97
19 The Straw-Man Argument 107
20 The Slippery Slope 113
21 Haste Makes Waste 119
22 Three Sneaky Moves 130
23 Part Two Review 142

Part Three   The Arguments 149

24 Pot Luck 151
25 The Gay Life 155
26 Equal Rights for Equal Arguments 159
27 Why Get Married? 164
28 Good-Bye, Friends 167
29 To See or Not to See 172
30 The Mark Market 176
31 To Therapy or Not to Therapy 179
32 Part Three Review 183

Appendix   Sources for More Information on
               Arguing Well 187

Index 191

Preface to the Revised Edition

I learned how to argue on the streets of Flatbush, in Brooklyn, New York. Being a "good kid" and not a "hood," I had to do something to keep from having my head knocked off every day. So it was that I discovered the power of persuasive argument. Later, at Hunter College (now Lehman College) in the Bronx, small gangs of us used to hang out in the halls throwing trick questions at unsuspecting profs. But when I went straight and began teaching I was shocked to learn that very few people really knew how to listen and respond to an argument. Finally I had a mission: to make the world more critical.

This book is an important part of my mission, and as such it must be understandable to the average reader. (What good is a mission no one can understand?) This book will show you how to argue and reason more effectively. It will also make you more aware of what is going on in an argument. I urge you to begin by reading Part Three and then to go back to Part One. Then when you read the whole book and go through Part Three for the second time you will be able to see and understand a great deal more. That will tell you for certain that the lessons learned in the book actually make a difference. This ability and your increased confidence can then be transferred to real arguments. All it takes is practice.

The preceding two paragraphs from the original foreword of the first edition still hold for me today. If anything, it is even more important that we all become adept at understanding and creating arguments. Demagoguery seems to be on the rise, and the media invade our minds with increasing skill and perseverance. Evermore we are presented with simplistic positions and addled arguments. The world seems to be breaking into opposing teams, and every team wants your allegiance. This book will enable you to choose wisely and carefully, and prevent you from being misled by fallacies and empty rhetoric. If I can increase your insight into and perception of the positions presented to you, and if I can decrease your gullibility and replace it with a healthy skepticism, then I will have succeeded in doing something important.

I am truly delighted that I won the argument with John Wiley & Sons, Inc. to re-issue *How to Win an Argument* in a new, revised edition. Of everything I have done, it is this book that seems to have stayed with my readers the most. I still encounter people who read the first edition 15 years ago who tell me how valuable they found it. So I am indebted to John Wiley and all his sons, as well as to my editor Judith

McCarthy and my agent Daphne Hart, all of whom saw that knowing how to argue well is a vital component of personal freedom and individual liberty.

This revised edition updates many examples, is rewritten for greater comprehension, and includes more pointers and tips. (Although there are a few old nuggets I could not bear to discard.) But the book keeps the spirit and feeling of the original that was so popular with readers. Throughout the text you will find displayed statements. These are either brief summaries of important points or tips for argument technique. They can serve as reminders and guides as you work through the material, and they will also serve as a quick refresher if you forget important elements. This revised edition also contains review exercises designed to insure that you grasp the important points and help you understand the material.

A great deal has changed in the academic field of Argumentation Theory since I wrote the first edition—in fact, the field barely existed then. Now it is a thriving arena of scholarship, with journals, conferences, courses, and competing approaches. Scholars from philosophy, communication theory, sociology, and psychology work together to understand this most important of human activities. I want to thank my colleagues around the world for their encouragement and kind words about this book.

It's still true that I recruited a multitude of missionaries along the way, many of whom stayed with me and continue to help. The impetus for the book came first from students in my courses and people at my talks and workshops, and this revised edition was urged upon me by many later students who felt cheated by *Win*'s unavailability. From them, the oldtimers, and the newcomers, I culled examples and insights. Many spent time looking through newspapers and periodicals for juicy fallacies, and the book is richer for their contribution. Like any missionary I was often overzealous and obsessive—in short, annoying.

To my many wonderful friends who put up with me, who read the book, and who have given me support and encouragement, I give my love. York University, a fine educational institution, also deserves thanks. Finally, I would like to thank Lisa, Chris, Paul, Rachel, my wonderful wife Diane, and my son Zachary, to whom this edition is dedicated.

Michael A. Gilbert
Toronto

PART ONE

The Art of Argument

1

What Are We Arguing About?

"I just don't want to argue about it."
"Don't argue with me."
"There's nothing to argue about, my mind is made up."
"Stop arguing and listen."
These expressions and others like them are thrown at us from childhood. Early on, in our most tender years, we are just not allowed to argue. Later, in school, an arguer is often labeled "troublemaker" or, at the very least, "uncooperative." Then, if you argue at work you're not "pulling with the team," or perhaps you're just plain "stubborn" and still uncooperative. Currently, we are being told that argument is not socially acceptable. Now you're not supposed to *argue* with people; instead you're expected be sympathetic, caring, and, above all, not hurt anyone's feelings—political or otherwise. This is especially difficult when dealing with the argu-

mentatively challenged. What is not clear is whether, after being emotionally sensitive and politically careful, can we then attack their arguments? No one seems to know.

With all this anti-argument propaganda it is no wonder that most of us argue so poorly. And this is the real problem: It is not *argument* that is objectionable, but *bad* argument that puts everyone off. We need to know the differences between good arguments and bad ones. A good argument shows what position a person holds, allows others to present their points of view, helps to reach and understand a decision, and does not tread people helplessly underfoot. The purpose of this book is to teach you about good argument—how to win one and how to experience the understanding, insight, and human contact that all good arguments engender.

Since very often the *truth* has little to do with winning or losing, the decision, even the "knockout," may go to the sneakiest or slickest viewpoint, and not to the best or wisest. It can be very frustrating to lose an argument from lack of expertise, experience, or confidence about *arguing*, and not because you were wrong. If the outcome is important to you (perhaps a raise or promotion is at stake), your frustration will be that much greater as you tell yourself that you should have won. You should have been able to make that point or defeat that objection. But you did not.

What went wrong? What reply might have worked? What did you miss?

In the following example Our Hero is stymied. Our Hero is trying to persuade a clerk to give him two forms so that he will not have to get on another line.

OUR HERO: May I have a form for my driver's license renewal and a form for my car registration renewal, please?

CLERK: Here's your license renewal. You can get your registration renewal two lines to the left, over there.

OUR HERO: Look, I've waited in this line for 20 minutes. All you have to do is reach 12 inches and get me a registration form. Come on, be a sport! I don't want to wait on another line.

CLERK: Sure. That's easy for you to say. But if I do it for you, I'll have to do it for everybody. Then I'll be running all over the place getting all sorts of forms. How can I do my job that way?

Instead of muttering under his breath and moving to the next line, Our Hero might have pointed out the weakness in the clerk's argument. Our Hero is not asking the clerk to run all over the motor vehicles agency—only to reach 12 inches. As for the clerk's fear that she will have to do the same for everyone (Why shouldn't she, if the task is so simple?), there is no question of her having to desert her post. She can do it all right there, on the spot.

Our Hero and the clerk are, in the broadest sense, having an *argument*. For many people that word brings to mind strong emotions, intensity, and a good deal of noise, shouting, and name-calling. Many arguments are like that. But in this book I will use the word *argument* to cover a much broader range of encounter.

*An **argument** is any disagreement— from the most polite discussion to the loudest brawl.*

So *argument* is a very broad word, including the many

different methods people use in their attempts to persuade or convince. Simple informal discussions and disagreements are arguments. So are the debates and confrontations that precede fights, battles, and wars. Arguments can be among the mildest of polite conversations, and they can be the most violent and lethal of exchanges.

Some people believe that arguments should always be crystal clear, unemotional, and devoid of drama and feeling. This view is wrong. An overly proper and correct argument is just like a very proper and correct party—a bore.

Many other people fear that they become too emotional when they argue, that they become excited, lose control, and in turn lose the argument. But there is no reason why you should not become emotional and involved; the trick is to *use* that emotion and involvement, and not let it stand in the way of good argument.

Most arguments are not presented in prim and proper form; they are presented in any way that might be convincing. Besides, trying to make arguments behave according to textbook rules destroys them as an art form, as a mode of expression and persuasion.

The desire for carefully laid-out arguments—the wish to see arguments as careful, precise, beacons of reason—is understandable. But who is so fortunate as to come across only such examples of perfection?

Day in and day out we read about or hear from those who make their livings by hoodwinking and cajoling (as is done by politicians and advertisers, for example). These people will not give up their bags of tricks simply because they hear a call to high moral standards. A far more promising hope is that the general public will arm itself with the skills of good argument. Then, if a politician commits a mistake during an argument, she will be caught and embarrassed, dramatically decreasing the use of shifty maneuvers. Unlike arming people with guns or bombs, no one will die from being armed with the techniques of argument. Instead, real communication will be increased through greater awareness of the complexities and subtleties of argument.

2

Why Argue So Much?

Why do we argue? Why do we make trouble? Why are we obnoxious and disagreeable? Why can't we just get along and not make waves? Because we are constantly faced with decisions. And in order to make good decisions, *it is vital to consider* the issues, and the relevant arguments and positions.

Arguing provides the opportunity for the parties involved to explore and probe one another's positions and claims. By arguing, you have a chance to examine exactly what your opposer's position rests on. Plastic shopping bags should be made illegal? Why? What rights are involved? Who will suffer and who will gain? Are there alternatives to making such bags illegal? What problem forced this particular solution? What are the consequences of keeping them legal?

When you argue about an issue, you do not have to disagree with a position in order to attack it; by arguing you might just want to test or explore the ideas presented. One major reason for arguing, then, is to learn: to explore, probe, and test a belief or point of view.

Sometimes you argue when you already have a conviction and want to persuade others of its value, but even more often you are the one being persuaded. You are virtually surrounded by constant attempts to convince you. When the daily newspaper editorial supports compulsory garbage recycling and offers arguments, the aim is to convince you, the reader. The same holds for all arguments and positions presented on television and radio. In these situations you do not have the opportunity to reply. You are presented with polished and convincing arguments but can't object. The argument is stated, and there it is; you can take it or leave it.

Other forms of argument designed to persuade are the advertising messages that reach us by way of commercials, jingles, posters, and billboards. The reasons presented for trying a product can be good, such as efficiency or low cost; or the reasons can be poor, such as the prestige you will acquire. The errors in reasoning found in advertising are repeated elsewhere, for example in politics. When Polly Politician says, "Unemployment may be reduced by as much as 22 percent in the next six months," she relies on the same "hedge-words" as an advertisement saying "Shine toothpaste may reduce cavities by as much as 36 percent." Both use the expression "as much as," indicating only an outside possibility, and both use the word "may" instead of "will."

When you want to convince someone that your view should be adopted, then you are arguing. If you suggest to a colleague, who wants to open a new branch office, that it might not be a good idea, you are also arguing. The colleague, at the same time, might aim to convince you that it is a good idea. In these situations you must be very quick.

Someone presenting you with a position expects either assent or disagreement. If you disagree, then there is a responsibility to explain why; if you cannot come up with a reason for your objection, then you are expected to agree. This forms a basic principle of argument, which will be discussed in chapter 8.

Arguing can also be fun, especially when not about something vital. Arguing is like playing—it is not only possible, but desirable, to appreciate on its own, without trying to achieve some other end. Arguing when nothing is at stake can be a valuable experience, like playing a friendly game of tennis to prepare for a tournament. You can take more risks on outrageous maneuvers, maybe try out a new shot. You'll be more at ease, and so can pay more attention to what you are saying and how you are saying it.

You can also learn a lot about people from arguing with them. First, you learn what they believe about the issue at hand and why they believe it. Second, from the way they argue you also learn about their values, their beliefs, and the ways in which they present them. You end up not only with insights into your argument partners' *positions*, but into your partners' entire worldview as well.

When you argue,
you examine your beliefs
and learn about your partners
and yourself.

A common old saying is that one should never argue about religion or politics. This is nonsense. You want your beliefs to be true, yet the adage warns us not to examine or test the most important and basic of them. Should these be left alone? No. In fact, these are just the beliefs you should examine most carefully. By spotting weaknesses, mistakes, and falsehoods in your own and other people's arguments, you stand a much better chance of holding to and acting on true beliefs. The advantage to this approach is success; making decisions on false beliefs can only lead to error and trouble.

3

Types of Arguments

Arguments can be categorized in various ways, but one way deserves particular attention: This is the distinction between what I call "creative" and "attached" arguments. An argument is **creative** when the arguers are willing to explore a position in order to determine its value, when you and your partner are willing to alter or reconsider a position if strong arguments are brought against it. An **attached argument** is just the opposite: You or your partner have a strong commitment to a position, an emotional or psychological stake in seeing one conclusion triumph. Many times this is understandable: You might, for example, be arguing for a raise or promotion—you want your point of view accepted, and that is all you care about—you are very attached to the outcome.

Attachment to positions becomes a problem when there is a strong difference of opinion. Since attachment means that opposers are unwilling or unable to change their minds, they tend to become stubborn and uncooperative.

They have no genuine desire to understand and deal with the opposing arguments. All that matters to them is holding on to their beliefs. No one enjoys having their beliefs knocked about, but most of the time we are willing to think about them and let them be probed. When an arguer cannot do this, then he is too attached to the belief.

When you know that your opposer is unreasonably attached to some belief, you should treat the argument differently. If your argument partner does not change his mind, you should not assume you have lost; in situations of attachment, *nothing* will change an opposer's mind. Arguing with a salesman about the value of a product, with a nationalist about the policies of her country, or a parent about the beauty of his child—all are arguments unlikely to end in agreement.

=====

Watch out for strong attachment—
both your own and your opposer's—
and go slow when you find it.

=====

I ran into an example of strong attachment not long ago when I was having a cappuccino at a local coffee bar. "You know," the owner told me, "I have the cheapest prices around."

"Well," I responded, "actually I stopped somewhere else yesterday, where the cappuccino was cheaper by 50 cents."

"Oh, but what is the quality of the coffee?" said the owner. "It's no bargain if the beans aren't the best."

This change of subject (from price to quality) was as clear as a flashing sign that the argument would go nowhere. Fortunately, I had no special interest in persuading the owner of anything.

In a creative argument both parties are more interested in finding the truth or solving the problem than in being right. When you argue creatively you are interested in your partner's arguments, and you listen to them carefully to see if there is helpful information or insights. Your partner is also listening to you, and you work together to come up with the best solution or correct answer. Creative argument minimizes the role of the arguers' egos and maximizes their commitment to inquiry. The result of a successful creative argument should be agreement that the optimum result was reached.

If you are arguing with someone who is strongly attached to a position, you cannot judge the outcome in the same way you judge a creative argument. Instead, you must carefully follow the line of reasoning, noting the weaknesses and strengths of the arguments presented without expecting to change your partner's mind. The same holds true if *you* are attached to a view. You might not want to publicly change your position at the time the argument is taking place, but you should try carefully to note the weak points of your own position so that you can shore them up, make them sharper, or strengthen them in some other way.

4

Defensive vs. Offensive Argument

The main thrust of this book is defensive. Just as defensive driving techniques teach you how to protect yourself against sloppy and dangerous drivers, here you will learn to defend yourself against bad arguments and tricky maneuvers. Many people only care about winning an argument. They want to change your mind and don't care how they do it. These are **offensive** arguers, and you have to know how to defend yourself against their tricks. Offensive arguers have only one goal: to get your agreement, vote, business, or support. Whether the argument is in the media where you cannot respond, or in a face-to-face interaction, it is vital to know how to defend yourself.

As you learn how to defend, you will also develop the skills needed to attack. By continually identifying maneuvers and tricks, you might also learn how to use them to your own ends. But a word of caution: People who use dirty tricks often defeat their own purposes by acquiring a reputation that arouses suspicion.

*The essence of
defensive argument is simple:
Assume everyone is out to get you!*

Most people you'll argue with want just one thing: agreement. And they do not care how they get it. Knowing this, you'll approach every argument with a highly skeptical, critical, investigative attitude—the prime requirements for a successful arguer. *Believe nothing.* The less you believe, the less likely you are to believe something false.

When arguing, always assume your opposers are both sharp-minded and low-minded; that way you'll never underrate their ability. Since many argument maneuvers are not made *consciously*, the simple fact that someone is sincere does not mean you can trust her arguments (though you might be able to trust the person).

Many people think their arguments are correct when they are really full of errors. Offensive arguments are not always intentional—nasty techniques and traps can happen accidentally. There are also people who are so sure they are right that any means of advancing their position is acceptable. Offensive arguers often have the attitude that "the end justifies the means." But while they are already convinced, you should not be. You want the straight goods, while they want to sell you a bill of goods.

Offensive arguing can happen in all innocence. We all know, for example, how hard it is to probe for and discover the bad aspects of something we think we may want. Suppose you are considering moving into a new neighborhood, so you chat with several residents and ask them what they do not like about the area. But they are convinced that *when all is said and done* theirs is a good neighborhood to live in. In situations such as these you need a defensive attitude to get the information you want so you can make your own decisions.

Defensive techniques are especially useful when it comes to defending yourself against advertising. After employing these techniques a while you will cease to believe *anything* you see, read, or hear in an advertisement. Catchwords, hedge-words, and unsubstantiated claims abound throughout advertisements that seem to promise much, but in fact offer little. Often ads are designed to suggest certain associations or connections that are totally false. Sometimes they feature sober-looking men in suits designed to inspire confidence; at other times they depict lovely men and women enjoying the very lifestyles we ourselves would like. Still other ads associate a product with fun and youthful *bonhomie*. These associations are made and fostered very purposely.

A current fad in advertising relies on the public's concern for the environment. Suddenly products once frowned upon may now be touted as "green," and not harmful to the planet. Investigation shows that these claims are controversial, some even causing turmoil within environmental groups themselves. What is really going on? Have the products really been changed, or just the advertising? Are the manufacturers' and retailers' sudden concerns for the environment genuine, a marketing ploy, or both? The difficulty in answering such questions is obvious, but the point is that you must learn to be highly skeptical about *all* claims until the proof is in.

There is no such thing as being too skeptical.

After paying careful attention to arguments for a short period of time, you will become trained to notice precisely what you are being told and precisely what you are reading. The exact claim made in an ad is often dramatically different from the claim that one might at first think is being made. Using defensive techniques, you will quickly spot these and other offensive arguments designed to mislead you. The point is this: The more suspicious you are, the less likely you are to be hoodwinked.

5

Some Warnings

When arguments are conducted properly they increase contact between people and afford a healthy form of interaction. But not all arguments are conducted properly: Strong attachment to a position often leads quickly to a loss of perspective and calm. Sometimes, too, it is not what the argument is *about* but whom the argument is *with* that is the cause of attachment. Arguing with any psychological rival—such as one's boss, teenager, spouse, or colleague—can lead to heated argument, not because of the subject but because of the relationships of the arguers to each other. You are probably familiar with fights between married couples or children and parents that are really about "nothing." These are arguments in which the ostensible reason for the fight hides a deeper issue. In these situations it is especially important to be careful that winning not be seen as just getting your way without regard for your partner's feelings or concerns. It is also terribly important to argue as creatively as possible by leaving yourself open to your partner's words and position, showing a willingness to change your mind, and not acting as if you are right and that's all there is to it.

In general, learn to judge how attached your opposers are to their positions. Also try to note how attached they are to winning. Some people do not especially care how they come out of an argument, but will still defend their position as best they can. Others seem to have a need to come out victorious. In all these situations try to judge just what is the benefit to you of pushing hard, and what the cost might be to your opposer.

---

*If an opposer is
very attached to a position
—and you are not—back off.
It's not worth it.*

If your respondent is strongly attached to a position, you will rarely get her to change her basic view. But, by going at it in bits and pieces, one move at a time, you may make slower but deeper progress. This means you may not make progress all at once, but over time and by paying careful attention to the details of the argument, you may see your opposer change her position.

This is a good time to raise another warning. Most of us have one or two issues on which we are inflexible. There may be one or two (hopefully not more) subjects on which we have an opinion which we will never really budge. What is more, every time we get into an argument on one of these topics, we argue very poorly and end up irritated. This happens to all of us. The topics can be anything, frequently themes with which we were raised, such as the liberation of the ancestral home. Basques discussing Spain, Estonians on Russia, or Jews on Israel often find it hard to be objective—it seems as if too much is at stake. Regardless of who is right and who is wrong, the issue is so emotionally alive for them that they cannot discuss it dispassionately, and may even have difficulty being reasonable. Most of us have blind spots such as these.

Come to know your blind spots and, when you are incapable of arguing reasonably, know that it is time to stop. If you maintain a position largely because of your upbringing or emotional involvement, how can you argue creatively? Your reason for arguing will be basically that you *want* to believe in the position, and no one is going to change your mind. But what kind of a reason is that? Positions are not true simply because we *want* them to be. Your attachment may prevent you from presenting good reasons for your position, and you will not be able to tolerate those reasons being probed.

Sometimes you cannot back off. If a belief involves others—if it touches on issues such as abortion or racial prejudices, for example—then you have a responsibility to investigate. So the answer seems to lie in being aware of your blind spots while at the same time trying, perhaps gently, to explore them. If you are careful and do not go beyond the point of risk or irritation, you may learn a great deal. And as you learn, the point of risk or irritation will become clearer; you will develop a finer sense of your own blind spots and perhaps begin to examine them critically.

The rule is to remember that your chances of changing someone's mind when he or she is deeply attached to a position are slight. It therefore makes sense just to try to make a dent in their position, by slow and careful exploration. If you can't change someone's mind, then at least try to sow doubts; then, at the next encounter you can try and move further.

One last warning is in order: The techniques in this book are fairly powerful. By the time you've finished this book, you will find it easy, at the very least, to confuse people who are not on guard. *Don't do it.* The techniques in the pages that follow are presented to give you a better idea of what you are up against. But, by learning how *you* can be deceived, you also learn how to deceive others. You can combat would-be deceivers by pointing up their deceptions. If you turn to deception, you are only increasing the number of deceivers. Socrates, remember, was put to death for (allegedly) making the worse argument seem the better, and the better argument seem the worse. His relentless attacks on the unquestioned beliefs of his day led to his extreme unpopularity with the authorities. Even though the penalties today are not nearly so severe, deception disguised as argument is still offensive.

Remember: Don't be obnoxious!

6

Super-Rule I: Never Admit Defeat

I've been talking all along about winning arguments. But what, after all, does it mean to "win" an argument? Do you imagine your opponent capitulating, giving in, and accepting your position? "Gadzooks, you're right! And all this time I was wrong. Thank you for showing me the light." Oh yes, sweet victory! But this rarely happens.

In many arguments, the topic under debate determines what "winning" means. If, for example, you are arguing about a yes-or-no situation, then in many cases the winner can be easily identified. If you are arguing about opening a branch office and it is in the end *opened*, the person who wanted it opened is the victor. But even in such a seemingly clear case as this, there may be compromises that mean there really is no crystal-clear winner.

Usually when you argue you do not get the sort of turnabout you might like. What you can often do, however, is plant seeds of doubt in the mind of your partner, shaking the foundations of his position or belief. Weeks later you might find your opposer has completely changed positions. And, while he may never admit it, the changes are likely due to the seeds you planted in the original argument.

If an argument is creative, then in one very important sense no one loses. A **creative argument** involves people who have a belief, hunch, or idea about the truth, but who are also open to change. The result of a creative argument either confirms a particular viewpoint or shows that it is incorrect. In either case you leave this kind of argument with more information than you had before. If you are not swayed, then you know at least that these particular arguments were not effective enough. On the other hand, your dispute partner may have planted seeds of doubt, or pointed out new difficulties in your argument, and this too is valuable.

No one really loses a creative argument.

In a creative argument, neither position is a clear victor. Yet the investigation, the examination of the issues and problems, provides insights and information about the position. In a creative encounter you always come out ahead—one very important kind of winning.

Here is a very important question that may come up in the course of an argument: What happens when you realize you are wrong? Your opposer has presented aspects of the problem you have not thought of, and at this time you cannot think of any reasonable reply. What should you do? Admit defeat and change the position? Admit that you cannot answer these points? Or, should you use some maneuver to cover your tracks and get out of the argument? This is a very important question, and the answer—Super-Rule I—is controversial.

> *Super-Rule I: Never admit defeat, unless you are absolutely convinced . . . and even then keep your mouth shut and wait 'til Monday.*

The rule means that you should never hastily concede defeat except in circumstances necessary to your well-being (to keep your job or save your marriage, for example). It is possible to admit defeat later, but at the time of argument it is almost always inappropriate to concede.

One reason for following Super-Rule I is very simple. In the vast majority of cases you do not argue about matters of fact but about matters of opinion. If the argument is about a matter of fact, it may be simply decided: There *is* an answer. If arguing about the capital of Saskatchewan, or the author of *For Whom the Bell Tolls*, for example, there is no need to continue once you check the right source. Look in an atlas or library catalogue to settle the matters simply. But most arguments are about matters of opinion. What is the best car to buy today? Is this a good time to expand our sales operations? Should Zachary be allowed to watch so much television? These questions do not have straightforward answers; even experts would disagree. One opinion has as much *initial* possibility of being correct as any other.

The purpose of most arguments, then, is to determine which side can hold up better under examination.

The key reason for using Super-Rule I is the desire to keep the investigation open. After all, if the purpose of the argument is to investigate a view under fire, to explore a position that is being pushed to its limits, then why give up? When someone concedes defeat the exploration stops. When that happens, the "winner" ceases considering the argument seriously and hearing the objections to the attack, and instead just savors the victory.

A second reason for Super-Rule I lies in our own limitations. You are each familiar with the jolt of thinking what you *should* have said in that particular discussion—but that perfect sparkling reply is too late. Admitting defeat on the spot means you are totally convinced you will never think of a great counter-argument. So, why not *postpone* your reply? There is absolutely nothing wrong with saying, "That's an interesting point. I am going to stop now, but assure you that I will consider your argument further." The nineteenth-century German philosopher Arthur Schopenauer wrote, in "The Art of Controversy,"

> The argument which would have been our
> salvation did not occur to us at the moment.
> Hence we make it a rule to attack a
> counter-argument, even though to all appearances
> it is true and forcible, in the belief that its truth is
> only superficial, and that in the course of the
> dispute another argument will occur to us by
> which we may upset it, or succeed in confirming
> the truth of our statement.*

---

*Arthur Schopenhauer, "The Art of Controversy," *Essays From the Parega and Paralipomena*, translated by T. Bailey Saunders (London: Allen and Unwin, 1951).

It is possible that what seems clear and convincing to you at one moment may not seem so credible later on. Not admitting defeat leaves open the possibility of continuing discussion.

Haste means you might admit defeat too quickly, and then it will not be long before you change your mind back to your original position. The responsibility is on you to think of the replies you need, or to finally agree to change your mind, but you need the time and context in which to do this properly. If you are a creative arguer, then you take losing an argument seriously—if it really means changing your mind, then you should not give up easily. By not conceding hastily you are giving your capitulation more respect and meaning.

A quick win is seldom durable.

You may find that many of those with whom you argue are better persuaders, speakers, and arguers than you are. Also, they may be attached to their positions and intent on persuading you at all costs. To admit defeat as a result of an argument with such a person is a form of unilateral disarmament. Super Rule I provides you with a healthy way to protect yourself from the tremendous amounts of hogwash constantly thrown at you.

Like anything else in this book, Super-Rule I does not apply across the board. (I could add a Super-Rule Zero: No Rule Applies All the Time. But this is something that should go without saying.) Sometimes, of course, you may realize you have simply made a mistake in reasoning. You may, for example, have thought your respondent's position on abortion implied that no killing was ever justified, but when questioned she clearly points out why that is not the case. In this kind of situation there is nothing wrong with retracting an objection. Caution should never be confused with stubbornness.

7

How Are Arguments Built?

We always argue, one hopes, about something: "We should expand the plant," or "When all is said and done we're still better off with a small car," or "Jimmy is much too young to go on an overnight trip without supervision." Arguments will surround such statements, and reasons will be given why they should be accepted or rejected. What's even more confusing is that you have to argue about the reasons. In order to minimize confusion you need to understand how arguments are built.

The statement describing the argument is the **claim** or the **conclusion**. Usually stated at the outset and identifying the topic of the argument, the claim is what the argument is about. It sounds simple, but it is amazing how often people do not know what they are arguing about. This is not only true of marital disputes running on more than one level, but also of less-attached arguments. An opposer's statements can easily lure you into following some track that leads in a completely wrong direction. If your opposer is asked why she is bringing in some unrelated point, she may well have no reply. And, if you do not catch that misleading maneuver, then the argument becomes like a swiftly running racehorse that turns off the course and onto a driveway: The horse is still running, but not in the race. This happens so frequently that I present the following rule.

Always know what you are arguing about.

This may seem like a silly rule, but what *is* silly is that we *need* such a rule. Experience shows, however, that the rule itself is essential.

It is very easy to find out what the argument is about: *Ask*. This is a good idea, since then you find out what you want to know, and also get your respondent's statement of the claim. Such a step provides crucial information: How is your opposer viewing the argument? When his claim is carefully restated, you can then recall what you think the argument was about. The differences between what you think and what the opposer thinks can be very important.

A very good way of getting out of an argument
you seem to be losing is to ask something like,
"What do you think we are arguing about?"
Whatever answer is returned say,
"Oh, I see. I thought you meant something else."

Another advantage to asking is that you gain time while your opposer formulates an answer: You might even ask *just* to get some time to think. If you're confused you can always ask to have the topic restated. Although sometimes your opposer will have no trouble providing an immediate, terse, and clear statement of the claim, more often she too will be confused and will have to think. This provides time for you to marshal a counter-argument.

If someone asks you to state the claim, especially if there is an audience—say, "I had a feeling you didn't know what we were arguing about. Why don't you try taking a guess?"

While the claim is the topic and focus of the argument, most of the time will be spent on the reasons for accepting or rejecting the claim. Every claim must be supported by reasons. **Reasons** answer the question, "Why accept this claim?" If the reasons are good, then you cannot effectively attack the argument. This is a basic key to understanding argument: If the reasons are good and the logic is correct, you are bound to accept the claim. This is why you never attack claims directly. If Paul and Caroline are arguing about what sort of car to buy, there is no value in each of them just stating and restating claims. Paul needs to dismiss Caroline's *reasons* for buying a sports car: for example, "They are not cheaper to own even though they are good on gas," he might argue, "because they are expensive to service." If Paul just responds with, "I don't want a sports car," he is only restating his claim and not advancing the argument.

Reasons are usually, but not always, the focus of an argument. Sometimes there is nothing wrong with the reasons, but the logic is not correct, so the claim just does not follow. Suppose Rebecca has suggested that Greene is a cruel murderer. Rebecca's opposer responds, "There is no doubt that Greene is the killer—let's hang the crumb!"

"Well, I agree," Rebecca may reply, "that Greene is the killer. But I can't agree that he should be hanged. That does not follow." Even though Rebecca agrees Greene is guilty, she points out that her opposer has not established the claim. It just does not follow only from what her partner said that Greene should be killed—and more argument is required.

---

*Always attack the **reasons** for a claim,
not the claim itself.*

When you provide a reason to back up a claim you must be prepared to defend it. You might state, for example, "We should get a sports car because they are cheaper to maintain." That is a reason that supports your claim: Buy a sports car. But when your opposer says, "What makes you think that sports cars are cheaper to maintain?" then your reason has been attacked and you must now defend it.

You might reply: "They are cheaper on gas because most have four-cylinder engines." This comment is to the point and is a reason for the reason. While this can go on forever, most arguments are self-limiting. Sometimes a point of common knowledge or agreement is reached, while at other times you may arrive at a point of fundamental disagreement. Separating reasons and claims, examining them carefully, will aid you in learning what are the crucial differences between you and your opposer. Knowledge about crucial disagreements is valuable; once it is known, the chances of reaching some consensus can be judged. How basic is the difference? Is it an irreconcilable difference? These are important questions.

8

The Principle of Rationality

Someone who believes something without reason is being irrational. In terms of argument, being rational means providing reasons for beliefs. In the end all of us may be irrational, since sooner or later we reach a point of ultimate beliefs (for which it is impossible to provide reasons). But at other times it is surprising how, with some thought and prodding, we can often go beyond even ultimate beliefs and provide rationales. The sequence of claims and reasons may even come back and meet itself, so that in the end your beliefs form a circle.

> *The Principle of Rationality:*
> *Always assume that people have*
> *reasons for their beliefs.*

Your willingness to argue with other people rests on the Principle of Rationality. I assume that if you believe something you have a reason, and you assume the same for me. By sticking to the Principle of Rationality, the following sort of dialogue does not occur:

"Let's get a sports car."

"Why?"

"No reason."

Your initial reaction on hearing this argument would be simple disbelief: There *must* be a reason—a silly reason, but a reason nonetheless—otherwise, why want a sports car at all? (People who do things without reason often find themselves under medical scrutiny.) The Principle of Rationality is necessary to argument since there is no point in arguing with someone who does not have reasons. The assumption is that you must always defend your positions and actions on request—without this assumption, communication and argument would come to a halt.

The Principle of Rationality states that you will be given reasons for a position, but it says nothing about their quality. There is no guarantee you will be given *good* reasons. In fact, reasons can be impulsive, whatever was thought of first:

"Why are you going to vote for Stevens?"

"Because my cousin went to high school with his sister."

That is hardly a good reason for wanting someone in office, but it satisfies the principle. The principle does not state you will be given the speaker's true reasons or motivation:

"Why do you want to be President, Mr. Jarvis?"

"Solely to serve my country."

Jarvis probably has other interests as well, but he need not present them to comply with the principle. The real reasons for wanting to be President or wanting to buy a sports car may have nothing to do with the stated reasons (a desire for a sports car rarely has much to do with economy and careful decision making). But arguers often hide their real reasons behind other, less embarrassing, reasons—a process called **rationalization** that shows how necessary the Principle of Rationality is. We always want to give reasons and, if we do not like the real reasons, we will make up others.

One sort of person often lacking reasons is a fanatic. There are two rules for dealing with a fanatic.

First Rule for
Dealing With a Fanatic: Don't!

But we all succumb to temptation. Fanatics are so easy to rile and excite that the desire to argue with them is often overwhelming. There are, however, two points to keep in mind: The first is that fanatics sometimes can provide useful information. Frequently they are quite well informed about their subject and can offer every standard argument. They tend not to go very deep, but they do frequently have an excellent grasp of the basics. The second point is the appreciation of the standard fanatic's argument. Generally, their arguments will run somewhat as follows—supposing our fanatic is a "triadist" (whatever that is, let Triadism stand for your favorite fanatic's position).

FANNY FANATIC: Triads are the essence of the universe. Everything comes in triples.

OUR HERO: What on earth does that mean?

FANNY: To properly understand the universe, you must see the triads.

OUR HERO: How can I see them? I don't offhand see anything that might be a triad.

FANNY: Ah . . . ! First you must learn to look and truly *see* the world.

OUR HERO: How do you know that the way *you* see the world is the "true" way?

FANNY: I know. Once you see it, you too will know.

OUR HERO: I disagree. I see the world just fine and think there's probably nothing else to see.

FANNY: That is only because your vision is clouded.

OUR HERO: How do you know *your* vision is not clouded?

FANNY: Oh, I know. I know.

Nothing will move Fanny. She is relying on a fallacy called **"special pleading."** She is claiming privileged knowledge, information available only to her. Anyone who disagrees with her is blind in some way. There is nowhere to go with the argument, since nothing—no facts or reasons—will be accepted by Fanny as evidence against her position.

This leads to our second rule for dealing with a fanatic.

=====

*Second Rule for
Dealing With a Fanatic: When stuck,
ask, "What would it take
to prove you are wrong?"*

=====

The second rule is a handy maneuver for any stubborn opponent unwilling to discuss reasons. Progress may not be made, but at least you can say you tried. Fanny just might reply to the question by saying that, if anything vital were shown to come in a pair instead of a triad, then she would have to reconsider. The difficulty then would be to find an acceptable pair. A good fanatic will be expert in showing why particular bits of counter-evidence are not relevant. Pointing out a pair like Love–Hate would undoubtedly bring the response that you have misconstrued the relationship . . . that it's really Love–Neutrality–Hate. (What is terribly interesting, but not to Fanny, is that Pairism is every bit as easy to defend as Triadism.)

The Principle of Rationality is vital to argument because if you are not provided with reasons, then you have nothing to attack. If the reasons for a claim are not good or real, they probably will not stand up very well. This means more reasons must be given, and then you may get closer to the truth. So even when the reasons given are not very good ones the Principle of Rationality still helps you slowly make progress.

9

Two More Principles

As described by the Principle of Rationality one major assumption we all make about our beliefs and positions is that we have *reasons* for them. Another assumption every bit as general and every bit as important to argument is that an arguer will be *consistent*. Without the assumption of consistency all argument would grind to a sudden halt.

Consistency demands that you have a reason not only for making a claim, but also for making distinctions in similar cases. If there are three children and you give them each a prize, no explanation is called for. But if you give just one a prize, then you must provide a rationale in the form of a **relevant difference**. The relevant difference might be obvious—the prize goes to the winner of a contest or to the best behaved. Whatever the reason, *regardless of whether it is a good reason or a bad reason*, we expect one.

Remember the motor vehicle clerk in chapter 1? She argued that if she got two forms for Our Hero, then she would have to do it for everyone—she would have to apply the rule consistently. Imagine a woman on the line behind Our Hero who sees him receiving two forms. Her turn comes, she asks for the same two forms, but she is refused. She would demand an explanation and, if none were forthcoming, would likely raise a horrible fuss. She would demand to know the relevant difference between her situation and Our Hero's.

One notorious example where relevant difference becomes crucial is in arguments about abortion. One of the arguments offered by those *against* abortion is that there is no relevant difference between a fetus and a newborn baby, that what applies to one must apply to the other. In other words, if a fetus has the same rights as a baby, it simply cannot be killed. (Nor could we put a pregnant woman in prison, but that's another story.) Since killing babies is acknowledged by practically everybody as immoral and criminal, a *supporter* of abortion, in order to treat a fetus and actual baby differently, must find a relevant difference between them. Needless to say, the sides do not agree on the relevant differences, but both sides agree on the *importance* of a relevant difference.

Another example concerns the U.S. Federal Bureau of Investigation (FBI): No U.S. citizen is allowed to do any number of things the FBI has done. Over the years, this has included sending fake threatening letters, illegal wiretapping, and general harassment of numerous groups. When challenged the FBI has offered in defense the argument that their function as guardians of national security provides the relevant difference between the restrictions on *our* behavior and the lack of restrictions on theirs. Sometimes, fortunately, depending on the political mood of the times, the U.S. Congress and courts have rejected the importance of this distinction.

The concept of relevant differences can now be restated as the Principle of Similar Cases.

> *Principle of Similar Cases:*
> *Where two cases or situations are*
> *similar, a reason must be offered*
> *for not treating them the same.*

This principle nicely complements the Principle of Rationality, which states that you will be given reasons for positions. The new principle makes it clear that reasons must be given for beliefs about differences in similar situations. Consider an argument about a stoplight at a meeting of the local neighborhood association. The argument is between Our Hero and a City Councilwoman:

OUR HERO: We need a stoplight at this corner. Children cross there all the time, and one of them is going to get hurt.

COUNCIL: That intersection is identical to hundreds of others in the city. Why should we put a light there and not at the others?

OUR HERO: This one is more dangerous than most.

COUNCIL: No, it's not. There have been fewer accidents at this intersection than at many others that don't have lights.

The Councilwoman is appealing to the Principle of Similar Cases. Why should this intersection be singled out? In a situation such as this Our Hero has only two choices. He can maintain that there *is* a difference and make a position for it, or he can agree that there is *no* difference. If he agrees that there is no difference, his best move is to maintain that *all similar* intersections have lights. His first choice might proceed as follows:

> OUR HERO: Of course, I'm sure you're right. And that's why we believe that *all* of these intersections should have lights. And we want to know what you are going to do about it!

Such arguments also utilize a third and final principle:

The Principle Principle:
Virtually every position
contains a general principle:
In everything there is a principle.

When the Councilwoman was told that a stoplight was wanted, she immediately drew out Our Hero's implicit principle or rule: Put stop lights in all similar intersections. Knowing the rule Our Hero is committed to, the Councilwoman can argue against it. She might point out that it is too expensive, that it would slow traffic too much, and so on. By extracting the principle implicit in Our Hero's position, she now has a handle on what she is fighting about.

Virtually every argument can be seen as one or both of two things. First, an argument over the truth of some principle; or, second, an argument about the application of some principle. It is not always easy to know what principles are at issue, but it is always important.

*Always know the principles to which
you are committed,
and always know the principles to which
your opposer is committed.*

Many jurisdictions are currently considering making the use of bicycle helmets compulsory. The greatest objection to this legislation is directed to the underlying principle that an individual's freedom should not be curtailed. The argument may center on whether or not this principle is true. But, on the other hand, the argument may concern whether or not this principle applies. To show this, you might argue that it is not personal safety, but the effect on others (through increased hospital costs, lost work hours and so on) that warrants the legislation. Now the principle concerns communal cost, not interference with personal freedom, so the principle that our freedom should not be curtailed without reason has not been violated.

Suppose you want to attack the new principle. The Principle of Similar Cases states: Cases that appear the same must be treated the same unless a relevant difference is found. The new rule says that a practice that will lower communal costs may be required by legislation. So, you might ask your opposer, what about compulsory exercise? Is compulsory exercise the same as wearing a bike helmet? Why not? If it is, your opposer must accept that position or give up the principle.

Always identify your opposer's principles. By looking at the positions and reasons you can figure out what the principle is. Just knowing that your partner is against mandatory helmet legislation is not enough. But when you know he is against it because it interferes with personal liberty, you can determine the rule: Personal liberty should not be curtailed. A person who is against abortion because it cheapens life holds a principle different from a person who is against abortion because God forbids it. While the claim is the same, the reasons are different. The first opposer is committed to the rule that what cheapens life is wrong. The second opposer believes the rule that what God commands should be obeyed. You would expect the first to be against war, while the second would have to consult religious authorities.

Identifying your opposer's rule or principle is the first step. The second is finding good examples. A good example is one that fits the principle but is rejected by your partner. Suppose your opposer favors compulsory helmet use because it cuts down on communal costs. The example involving compulsory exercise is a good one: If all people had to work out or jog, communal hospital costs would go down—therefore the principle applies. But few people would want to support compulsory exercise legislation, so a difference must be found between helmet-wearing and exercise. If it is not found, the principle must be changed: The principle leads to both helmet-wearing and exercise—so the principle must go. On the other hand, if your opposer is willing to accept compulsory exercise, the principle stays, and you have to look for a different example.

The last option is for your argument partner to find a difference between the two. Perhaps bicycling is a privilege, while not having to exercise is a right. In this case the rule does not lead to both cases, so there is no problem for your opposer. Again, you look for a different example.

Suppose you are arguing against any sexual discrimination in hiring. Your principle is that anyone qualified for a job should be able to get it. Your opposer is trying to come up with examples where you would not want to apply the Principle of Similar Cases. She might try to stymie you with: "What about women football players? Should women be able to try out for the defensive line of the Giants?" If you say no, you must give up the principle or say why this case is different.

But, since you pay attention to your arguments and you know what rules you are committed to, you are not thrown off your pace by her counter-example of women football players: "Sure. If they can compete, more power to them. They ought to be able to try. There's already been at least one woman professional hockey player. I don't know if a woman would make it in football, but that's not the point. It's the opportunity, not the job, that concerns me."

Whenever possible, embrace the consequences of your position.

This means you are better off accepting the odd and unanticipated consequences rather than changing the principle. Arguing that examples are not similar or changing the rule can be dangerous—you might shift to a position you have not clearly thought out. If the example can be dismissed as different, there is no problem. But if not, try to hold onto the principle by accepting the example.

10

Super-Rule II: Listen!

People rarely listen to each other. Most of the time they should be listening, they are doing something else, like imagining what they are going to say next.

Super-Rule II: Listen!

This rule should never be forgotten or neglected. Failure to pay attention to it leads to disaster. All of us have had the experience of explaining a position or belief to someone very carefully, only to realize that he has not heard a word. This, above all else, is the most difficult obstacle to effective communication in argument: Failure to listen.

The value of listening carefully cannot be overemphasized. In the first place, the shock value—when your opposer realizes that you have heard her claim and listened to the reasons for it—will stand you in good stead. Many people step back in astonishment at the realization that it is *their* argument that is being addressed. Instead of the usual "you say your piece—now I say mine—now you say yours," your ability to respond with a comment indicating that you *heard* your partner will have great effect, sometimes throwing them off through sheer surprise.

In normal conversation, listening is nice but not critical. In many conversations, like the following, it is not even expected:

> CHRIS: I just got a new car. A Jeep.
>
> PAUL: Oh, yeah, they're great! I had one about eight years ago.
>
> CHRIS: I got a great price on it. The owner is going abroad.
>
> PAUL: Mine was a hand-me-down from a cousin, believe it or not.
>
> CHRIS: It's amazing on dirt—just goes anywhere! Last week we drove right up a half-mile hill on bare rock.
>
> PAUL: Yeah. I remember taking mine out to the beach all the time. . . .

There is nothing wrong with this conversation. Chris and Paul want a chance to talk about their respective Jeeps. There is no special need for either to listen intently. Paul fondly reminisces, while Chris excitedly talks about his new car. Conversations about cars, holidays, movies, books, and so on are often the same because nothing much is at stake. All the participants really want to do is tell some stories and chat a bit.

When you enter into an argument, however, the situation changes. In an argument, understanding exactly what is being said is crucial to successful communication. It is impossible to really persuade someone who has an opinion without listening to him or her very carefully. Only by hearing the claim and identifying the reasons that support it are you able to discuss or attack the position. And only by showing that the arguments do not work can you win.

The same holds true if you are defending a position. Unless you can show that your respondent's objections are wrong, you will not convince him. If you meet his every objection you might make some progress. Both attacking and defending a position require that you pay careful attention to what is being said. Arguing without listening is like driving with tunnel vision: You can only see where you are going, not where anyone else is.

Listening provides the fuel for the engine of argument.

Knowing the rules and gambits of argument is important, but it is impossible to use these tools if you are not listening. It is a rare argument that does not contain some mistake or a weak point, but you will only notice it if you are listening when it comes.

The world's greatest nonlistener to date was a teacher I encountered at a parents' meeting not long ago. This amazing individual, in charge of the meeting, was agitated that no parent had volunteered to help supervise school activities the following Monday. Parents were being harangued and exhorted. And it took three people six attempts to get through to the nonlistener that there was no school on that Monday! (I shuddered to think how the children fared in his classroom.)

Everyone fails to listen *sometimes*, but dealing with hardcore nonlisteners is especially difficult. You might get excited or abstracted and soon you're not paying as much attention as usual. But some people find it almost impossible to listen. In these cases repetition is the only thing that works. In an argument, unless the opposer is terribly long-winded, *do not interrupt*; wait patiently until she has finished and then politely say, "I'm sorry. You did not hear my point. Let me try again. . . ." This may not work. Your partner might once again go off on a little trip of her own without paying the slightest heed to your comments. Now you interrupt, apologize, and say something like, "You're missing my point. Look, you said _____ then I said _____ So, you now must explain how you will deal with my objection."

> *The only way to deal with a nonlistener is with patience and repetition.*

Even this last attempt may fail. But take solace: The true nonlistener suffers a lonely fate—no one wants to talk to him.

11

Zen and the Art of Argument

Many people are quick to say they are illogical (whatever that might mean), but very few people are truly illogical (and most of those are locked up).

*Being illogical does not mean
one is creative; being illogical
means one is crazy.*

People who claim to be illogical, usually with some barely hidden pride, are making a simple mistake: You can discover a conclusion any old way, but you can only convince someone else with reasons. Leaping to a conclusion does not make us illogical, just *intuitive*. When asked why you believe Harry is ruthless, you will usually—if you keep at it—be able to tell. What you do then is think backwards and follow the *path* of the intuition. If someone disagrees with your insight, then you are forced to defend it, give it up, or just go away. But there is nothing illogical about insights or intuitions.

We are all, like it or not, logical. And by reading this book you are getting better at logical argumentation by learning the tricks and gambits used by those who would, consciously or not, manipulate you. Some of you might be confounded by the quantity of new information, and you might be wondering, "How can I think of all this stuff and still argue?"

In the ancient Buddhist religion of Zen the highest achievement in every art and skill comes from a combination of knowledge and focus. Whether it is painting, flower arrangement, or archery, the method is the same. If you borrow this insight and follow the Twofold Path of Argument, you will become an accomplished arguer.

The *first* path of the Twofold Path is that of knowledge. To increase your power and ability you must increase your knowledge of what can be done in arguments. That is the purpose of this book: to provide you with information in such a way that it is natural and manageable. There is not a great deal to learn. Nothing I've explained so far should be new—it is just being made explicit. What was relied on unwittingly before is now conveniently laid out. In this fashion you have an opportunity to know what you are doing and what is being done to you. You have a better idea of what to expect, where to go, and why you are going there. That knowledge will make your arguments more effective.

There is, however, this problem of keeping all this new information in mind, of thinking about it when *ar-*

guing. How is that possible? You cannot *both* listen *and* think about Principle Whatever at the same time—Super-Rule II prohibits doing both.

This, then, leads to the *second* of the Twofold Path: pushing all of this information away and just listening. Like trying to remember someone's name, the harder you try, the more difficult it becomes; but, as soon as you give up, relax, and stop trying, the name comes to mind. This is how the Twofold Path works: The information is there, you have been accumulating it; by relaxing and listening, you allow the mind to react freely to what is heard. A similar situation exists in sports. You can learn all there is to know about the correct tennis or golf swing, but *thinking* about the right arm while on the court or links is the worst thing you can do. Instead, a coach will recommend you relax completely and clear your mind.

The Twofold Path of Argument:
The first path is learning the tools and moves;
the second path is concentration and relaxation.
One without the other does not work.

The references to Zen are only partially in jest. Clearing your mind and allowing your knowledge to work is no jest—it is the essence of Zen. Argument may seem complicated and confusing, but its actual practice must be simple if it is to be effective: Responses must take split seconds. Even a philosopher does not listen to a colleague's argument and then ponder for ten minutes before responding. Instead, responses are fairly immediate, and as the temperature of the argument increases, so does the tempo of response.

There is no great trick to learning to argue; it comes, like anything else, with practice. At first there is a need to refer more and more to the information; but this stage does not last long. Soon, even if you do not remember names and labels, you will be able to describe what your opposer is doing wrong. What does the name or label matter? Your partner will not be impressed unless she too is familiar with the name. So the important information is contained in the moves and principles, not in their names.

The answer to the question "How do you think of all that stuff and argue at the same time?" is that you do *not*. Do not *think* about arguing—just listen, argue, listen, argue. . . .

12

Part One Review

QUESTIONS

Answer these questions to see how much you've absorbed from Part One.

1. What are the most important parts of an argument?

2. Who can you trust in an argument?

3. How often do people argue?

4. How would you argue with someone who states, "I am against execution by hanging for capital offences?"

5. Why is the Principle of Similar Cases so important to argumentation?

6. How often is Super-Rule II—Listen!—violated?

7. When *shouldn't* we argue?

8. Is Super-Rule I—Never Admit Defeat—true?

9. Using the Principle Principle determine what is the implicit rule in the following argument: "Of course the monarchy is a good thing, it's been around for 1,000 years."

10. Do I have to argue, listen, and think about the rules—all at the same time—to become a good arguer?

ANSWERS

1. There are two basic parts to an argument. The first is the *claim* (or the conclusion) and it tells you what you are arguing about. The second are the *reasons* and they tell you why you are arguing about the claim. Make sure you understand both before you commit yourself to a position.

2. *No one.* Someone who disagrees with you may intentionally or unintentionally use a fallacy or other misleading move. Someone who agrees with you may have completely different reasons.

3. *Very often.* Much of what is considered ordinary conversation is really argument. Any time there is any disagreement—no matter how mild—the rules and procedures of argument come into play.

4. *You wouldn't.* Never argue against (or for) a conclusion without getting the reasons first. The speaker may be against hanging because he prefers boiling in oil!

5. The Principle of Similar Cases states that we will be consistent and that we will treat situations that are alike in the same way. Without such a rule we would never know what people were going to do, say, or think. Being consistent

requires arguers bring all their beliefs and attitudes into alignment and keeps them from being unreasonable.

6. Sorry, what was that you said?

7. There are two main situations: first, when you do not know what you are talking about. In that case, just be quiet and try to get information. Secondly, when the person with whom you are arguing is much more emotionally involved than you are. In this situation be very careful—you can hurt someone badly without intending to.

8. *Of course not.* There are times when it is perfectly appropriate to say that you are wrong—just be sure, that's all.

9. The argument has within it the general rule, "Things that have been around for 1,000 years are worthwhile." This principle would also cover quite a few items besides royalty, such as cancer, poverty, and fascism.

10. *No.* You just have to listen carefully. One good way to practice is to listen to *both* sides of an argument when you are not involved. Sit back and pay attention to who is saying what to whom. Notice carefully who is listening, who is being irrelevant, and who is committing fallacies.

PART TWO

The Ways of Argument

13

What's Going On Here?

Arguments are sometimes lost for a perfectly good reason: Your partner is right and you are wrong. But this, really, is the exception rather than the rule. Most arguments are not about subjects where right and wrong or true and false are clear. If an argument is about the weather, one person might be right and the other wrong. But if the argument concerns the opening of a new branch plant in Weehawken, a choice of summer camp for Sophie, or the fairness of a Supreme Court decision, then there is no simple, correct answer. Usually the better argument will triumph.

Since we are talking about arguments and not Truth, a whole raft of items become relevant. How well the case is presented, how well the position is known, how much thought has been given, how attached you and your argument partner are, the relationship between those involved—all become factors affecting the outcome. An argument, for example, between two friends about baseball will have a very different character and feel from an argument between a boss and employee about proper business procedure.

In many arguments there might be moves that make a case *seem* stronger than it is. They are traps. They appear to be innocent statements, when in fact something—or any number of things—has gone wrong. The subject of the argument might have been changed; alternative answers to the problem might have been sneakily limited; a source of information might have been unfairly dismissed. These are but three of a slew of tricky maneuvers common to arguments. The traditional name for such mistakes is **fallacies**: traps that look like a reasonable part of the argument but actually conceal some unfair maneuver.

---

*A fallacy may look good,
but its beauty is a trap.*

Watch Our Hero fall for a classic fallacy.

> OUR HERO: The whole question of execution as capital punishment is very tricky.
>
> JOSH: Tricky? How is it tricky?
>
> OUR HERO: Well, for example, I was just reading an ad yesterday placed by the Association of Prison Guards. The ad pointed out that prisoners serving life terms cannot be punished any more severely than they already are.
>
> JOSH: Well, what's so tricky?
>
> OUR HERO: The guards are afraid that prisoners already serving life terms can kill prison guards

without further punishment—they have nothing to lose. That would scare me if I worked in a prison.

JOSH: Oh, sure. But look, the only reason the guards are concerned is because of their job safety. What else do you expect them to say? They're prison guards, so of course they're going to argue for executions. Give me an argument from someone without such a vested interest and I'll listen.

OUR HERO: Well, I suppose they do have a vested interest, and no one else has given any good arguments that I've seen. I suppose you're right.

Josh has committed the fallacy of **attack on the person.** Instead of arguing about what the guards said, he addressed their interest in the outcome. Sometimes this information might be relevant but it is not grounds for rejecting the argument. Our Hero has fallen for a very ancient trap.

What about Josh? Is he nasty? Underhanded? A cheat? Who knows? People who commit fallacies can do so by accident or on purpose. When Polly Politician does not answer a direct question it is probably intentional. Josh, on the other hand, may very honestly believe that his reason for rejecting the guards' argument is a good one. (We can hope that Josh and Our Hero read this book.) Many fallacies are committed without any malice at all. When trapped in an argument, people say whatever will get them out of trouble—it's hard to fix blame in these cases.

Be careful:
The nicest people can use
the nastiest fallacies.

Instead of worrying about guilt, you can learn how to handle fallacies when they appear in arguments. Our Hero could easily have answered Josh by pointing out that the guards' argument might be offered by someone else without a vested interest, and then what would Josh say? So instead of laying blame, we will concentrate on handling fallacies.

Each of the following sections discusses one or more fallacies. For each one, several examples are given, and there are instructions for countering the fallacy or getting around it. Finally, there are general hints throughout.

I urge you to search out fallacies in your daily newspaper and in conversations. Like any other skill, you must practice consciously before the reactions and responses become automatic. Keep looking for examples of fallacies, and please send the best ones along to me—I collect them.

14

Ring Around
the Argument

MATTHEW: This book I just bought is great. I'm going to make a million because of it. It sure is a good buy!

LAUREN: How do you know you'll make a million?

MATTHEW: Well, look. It says right here on page three that you'll make a million if you follow the instructions. I can't lose.

Matthew, as we all know, will not make a million through the advice in the book. (The only ones who will profit from the book are the author and publisher.) What is more important, the argument Matthew gives Lauren is less than ideal. Here is another in the same vein:

> This guitar is very expensive and rare. It's handmade, and there are only two like it. If you don't believe me, ask the guy who sold it to me.

And one more classic:

> Of course we know that God exists. It says right in the Bible that God exists, and the Bible must be true since it's the Word of God.

Whether or not Matthew makes a mint, the guitar is rare, or God exists, the arguments have something in common: The reasons are only convincing if the *claim* is already taken to be true. But this kind of reasoning is a fallacy since the truth of the claim—the conclusion of the argument—is just what we are arguing about. In argument you never use the conclusion to prove the premise—it's always the other way around. If everything Matthew's book says is true, then he will make a million. But the book itself is hardly a place to look for reasons to believe it. It's like someone who says, "I'm really an honest guy. If you don't believe me, just ask me. I'll tell you the truth."

This fallacy is known by several names. The most familiar are **circular reasoning** and **begging the question**, but there is also the learned-sounding *petitio principii*. All allude to the central nature of the fallacy: The reasoning goes in a circle. One of the reasons is acceptable only if the conclusion is true, so the reason can hardly be used to support the conclusion.

The argument presented above for the existence of God is not that far-fetched. I once had a discussion with a book-selling Hare Krishna devotee that went something like this:

SKEPTIC: What makes you think that what this copy of the *Bhagavad-Gita* you are selling says is true?

PEDDLER: My Guru says so, and he is a true guru.

Reasons are presented to support claims. Since you are arguing about the claim you need to have reasons for accepting or rejecting it. Sometimes one of the reasons means the same thing ("comes down to the same thing") as the claim. If there is disagreement about the claim, there must also be disagreement about any statement that means the same thing. So, if you accept a reason that means the same thing as the claim, you have been tricked.

We argue about claims by examining reasons.

Another example of circular reasoning involves random testing. Often when a factory receives a shipment of something like ball bearings, tests are run to determine that the bearings do not have too high a failure rate. Since the factory receives thousands of bearings at a time, they cannot test them all. Instead, batches of ten are tested at random and, then, perhaps another ten batches of ten. In this way the factory can judge what the rest of the bearings are like. An engineer in charge of such an operation explained this to me, and it made a good deal of sense. But he went on:

> If the first bearing of a batch of ten failed to pass the test, then that batch was thrown back in and another batch was chosen. The reason is that the highest failure rate expected is one in several thousand, so if the first bearing selected fails, the test will likely not accord with the expected results. In other words, the failure rate for this batch will be too high.

This is blatantly circular, but not uncommon in statistics; it is circular because testing by random choice is supposed to determine the failure rate. But instead of using the test to determine the failure rate, the *expected* failure rate is being used to determine the validity of the *test*. Everything has been turned upside down. (And, oh, the engineer worked at a nuclear power plant.)

---

*An argument is **circular**
or **begs the question** when
one of the reasons assumes
what it is supposed to prove.*

Another interesting example of begging the question involves a discussion of changes to the welfare rules to require people on welfare to work. One reason given by one commentator was that a just society does not penalize people for being poor. Is that statement circular? Why does it beg the question? Well, how would anyone in favor of the changes react to the statement that a "just society" does not make people work for welfare? Surely someone arguing in favor of the changes must think they *are* just. In fact, the justice of the rules and the society that creates them is what the argument is all about.

Be very wary of evaluations such as "just," "good," "right," and so on in an argument. They frequently indicate a circular argument. They may occur with other reasons that are not circular, but they tend to bolster an argument in an unfair way. In the following example there are noncircular reasons as well as a circular one:

> POLLY: You should vote for me next week. I am sincere, honest, and forthright. I support lower taxes and higher benefits. I am, what's more, the best candidate. Vote for Polly!

Forthrightness, honesty, and sincerity are valuable (though rare) traits in a politician, and provide, if true, reasons to vote for Polly. But what you are trying to determine in listening to speeches is who is the best candidate. Polly's announcing that she is the best begs the question: You want to know *why* she is the best.

The form of the fallacy of circular reasoning is the same in relatively subtle cases, like most of those above, or in more blatant cases like these two:

Example A

LISA: I think women should have equal rights.
JOSH: You think so, huh? Well, I say it's crap!

Example B

JOSH: The candidate says she'll lower taxes.
LISA: That's nonsense and you know it!

In both examples the response begs the question. The simple assertion that a view is wrong is inadequate. Unless reasons are given for the rejecting the claim, the fallacy is committed. Sometimes, however, reasons do follow the claim's dismissal, and then no fallacy occurs: If Lisa goes on, in Example B, to explain *why* she believes the candidate will not come through, she is not committing a fallacy. Usually, though, summary rejections like "Nonsense!" are not followed by reasons, but left as is, in which case the fallacy is committed.

Another slightly different form involves labeling a view and then dismissing it because of the label. A common example finds a respondent throwing out accusations of "creeping socialism" or "more government subsidies," when that is exactly what is at issue.

SOPHIE: I think it's important that pregnant women receive special allowances for food.

DIDI: That's just another instance of creeping socialism.

Indeed, perhaps it is. Sophie will not disagree that state support is what's wanted. But we often fear and argue against the label rather than the issue. If Sophie goes on to maintain that it is *not* creeping socialism, she may, in the end, convince Didi; but Didi may still be against the support, regardless of whether or not it is socialistic. Instead, Sophie should stay on track and not be misled into an argument about labels:

SOPHIE: Look, Didi, call it what you want. I don't care if it's Socialism, Fascism, or Sufism, I think it's important because _____.

Now Didi must deal with the *reasons* Sophie has given. Didi's attempt at begging the question has been foiled.

Reasons and points may hurt your position,
but names will never harm you:
Don't fight about labels unless you must.

Avoiding arguments over labels is useful in response to statements like "Nonsense," "Rubbish," and so on. Generally an arguer, using a harsh response like that, will feel fairly strongly about the issue. But you should respond to name-calling dismissals like "Rubbish" in this way: "Perhaps. You may be right. But why do you think the view is rubbish?" A true question-begger will respond with more nonreasons like, "I know rubbish when I see it." But stick to it. With perserverance you may force the name-caller to present a *reason*able argument.

> *Treat a dismissal like "Nonsense!" as*
> *a claim and not as an argument.*

When the subtle form of circular reasoning occurs, you can turn the tables by using a similar approach. The effect will be the same: You force the opposer to treat the fallacious reason as a *conclusion*. In cases where a simple "Why?" will not suffice, the strategy is simple: Since the problem is that one of the *reasons* assumes too much, demand a justification for that reason. Since a conclusion cannot stand as a justification for the reason, demand a new reason be brought in. You know, but your opposer may not, that you are really still arguing about the original conclusion; you just changed the wording.

> *When the circularity is not blatant,*
> *identify the circular reason and*
> *demand that it be justified.*

OUR HERO: It seems to me that the abortion laws ought to be loosened.

ZACK: By no means! That would be awful. How can you even think such a thing?

OUR HERO: Well, it seems to me that a lot of harm is being done to women who cannot get abortions.

> zack: But how can you support murder? Every
> known society has rules and taboos against
> murder. Shall we be the only society that licenses
> murder?

Our Hero has to think fast. Zack's last comments are powerful and emotion-laden. How can he answer Zack's question? Who approves of murder? Our Hero is not stuck—he knows what the problem is: Zack has begged the question—the argument is about the legitimacy of abortion. If abortion is legitimate, it is not murder; if it is not legitimate, it is murder—that is what the argument is about. Our Hero responds:

> Frankly, Zack, it's not at all clear to me that
> abortion is murder. How can you be so sure?

The argument is still about the same thing, the rightness of abortion, but now the conclusion has changed from "abortion laws ought to be loosened" to "abortion is not murder." The important thing is that Our Hero knows what he is arguing about and so has been able to get round this circularity.

One last point: If the situation involves an audience, Our Hero might choose a slightly different maneuver. Depending on how obvious the fallacy is, he might point it out. If it is blatant, his opposer can be made to look foolish or sneaky. For example, Our Hero might have responded like this:

> Good Lord! You can't call it murder. That's what
> we're arguing about! What are you trying to do?

Such a move can be applied to all fallacies, not just circular reasoning. However, you must be convinced that the audience will see it clearly. If not, you stand the risk of getting involved in a confusing explanation.

*Pointing out fallacies can make a rival look foolish
or sneaky, but be certain
that your audience will see it immediately.*

Circular reasoning or begging the question is a common fallacy, but it can be beat. The surest way to beat it is to know your position. Red herring might be nice for breakfast, but in an argument it ends up tasting like crow.

15

What Were We Talking About?

One of the most common maneuvers within arguments is also one of the most infuriating. You're going along just fine, following and responding to your partner's arguments, when all of a sudden you feel like you just walked into a strange conversation. Somehow there has been a jump or switch that was missed, and you are overcome by a vague feeling of confusion. In many cases you find you no longer disagree, but your opposer is still arguing. When this occurs there has often been a **change of subject**; this fallacy, changing the subject, is also called *non sequitur*, irrelevant reason, or (ready?) *ignoratio elenchi*. Here I will call it "changing the subject," since that is the form that is most irritating and confusing—as illustrated in the following dialogue:

> OUR HERO: I thought, Polly, that you were not going to support an increase in taxes if you were elected.

POLLY: That's correct. I did not then anticipate such a need.

OUR HERO: But yesterday you voted for an increase in school taxes. Why?

POLLY: A politician must sometimes make unpopular decisions.

OUR HERO: But why this one?

POLLY: You wouldn't want me *not* to vote for taxes just so I might get re-elected, would you? Do you think an elected official should only do the popular thing?

OUR HERO: No, of course not. But what I don't see is. . . .

POLLY: Well, this was one of those times when I had to put the good of our children above my personal ambitions. I'm sure we all agree that our children deserve the best of everything.

If Polly were at a press conference, she would now smile and call for the next question.

Polly has eluded Our Hero by changing the subject. He asked her about a particular vote, seemingly in violation of an election promise. Her answer was irrelevant: that a politician must sometimes do the unpopular thing. We already knew she voted that way, so Our Hero's next question was "Why?" Notice how Polly presented her response in such a way as to elicit agreement: Yes, the taxes are unpopular, but are the taxes worthwhile? Polly would be expecting agreement on the statement that a politician must follow her conscience, but would not be upset by disagreement, which would set the argument on another course; Our Hero would end up arguing on a subject Polly had chosen. Why should an opposer change the subject to something as dangerous as the original subject, namely the difference between her campaign promise and her vote? Surely, she could go to something safer.

Here is another example of changing the subject:

DIDI: Frankly, I think the schools should be closed. Children don't learn anything worthwhile there anyway.

JOSH: I think you're being too extreme. They learn something. And it's the responsibility of society to see that children are educated. Surely you agree that it is our responsibility.

DIDI: Of course we have that responsibility. But it's not being fulfilled by the schools.

JOSH: Nonetheless, it is a very important responsibility and we should think very carefully of how we are going to fulfill it. After all, our children are our future. Aren't they the most vital aspect of our future?

DIDI: Of course, they are terribly important. That's why I want to close the schools.

Didi is giving Josh a run for his money. Josh wants to change the subject to the value of children, but Didi is keeping it on schools by quick agreement and repetition of her initial claim. By doing this, she can keep control of the argument and, with any luck, force Josh to deal with her position.

When suddenly you no longer know
what you are arguing about,
check to see if the subject was changed.

The subjects that crop up as safe havens for harried opposers frequently include the wonders of children, the importance of the family, and, of course, patriotism. Here Lisa is ready to have a go with Josh:

LISA: It would be awful if the government spent all that money for helicopters right now. They probably will never be adequate, and we have far more pressing needs at this time.

JOSH: But, surely they are vital for defense—the generals all say so.

LISA: Phooey. Those copters are no more vital to defense than I am.

JOSH: You *are* vital to defense. Isn't this a democracy?

LISA: Of course, what's that got to do with it?

JOSH: In a democracy everyone is vital to the nation—everyone has an equal voice. Don't you think that's the way it should be?

LISA: In fact I do. But I don't believe everyone does have an equal voice, and you're naive to think so.

And they are off and running! Josh has had better luck this time than he did previously with Didi. Having safely changed the topic (helicopters), he can freely agree with Lisa that it is a pity not everyone has an equal voice; but he will never have defended his position on helicopters. Lisa, however, committed a cardinal sin: She forgot what she was arguing about. She could have short-circuited Josh by *not* answering his question about democracy. She could have said something like, "It doesn't matter if this is a democracy or not. Right now is a bad time to invest in expensive helicopters."

To avoid being caught by a change of subject, know what the argument is about, listen very carefully, and be sure of your own position. After all, if *you* are confused or unclear as to your own position, you can hardly accuse an opposer of changing the subject.

If you do not know what the topic is, you cannot expect your opposer to stay on it.

Again, the best way to combat a particular fallacy is to know what you are doing. If you have a clear idea of what should be going on, you will know the moment your opposer leaves the track.

For a long time seat-belt legislation was a popular topic of debate. Should we be required by law to wear seat belts? Or is it a matter of personal choice? Do governments have a right to tell us what to do on this matter? In an argument I once read, an opponent of seat-belt legislation attacked it on the ground that alcohol is the major cause of accidents. The defender of the legislation fell for it and began arguing about alcohol. He was simply not quick enough to realize the subject had been changed.

Every summer many sports magazines have a swimsuit issue. The issue is not dedicated to an analysis of what swimwear is best for racing or scuba diving, but rather it is an opportunity to increase sales by displaying a large number of scantily clad women. There have been protests made arguing that these displays have nothing to do with sports and are sexist—and "pornographic"—to boot. The publisher of one major magazine replied to a reporter, "Our magazine is not porno. I've got an eight-year-old son and he looks at it."* What is interesting about his answer is that it is probably true. But what does his son's reading habits have to do with the legitimacy of the contents of his magazine? Nothing at all.

During the late-1980s U.S. national debate over cigarette smoking, another *non sequitur* occurred in a letter to the editor complaining about Surgeon-General C. Everett Koop's irritation at cigarette ads. The writer of the letter insisted Koop not be taken seriously until he also complained about beer ads.† Perhaps the Surgeon-General should have complained about beer ads, but what is the connection to cigarettes and their advertising? None.

The reporter interviewing the swimsuit magazine publisher, or Lisa, or Our Hero should have obeyed Super-Rule II: They should have listened very carefully and noticed the change in subject. For most arguers, however, constant obedience to Super-Rule II is too much to ask. Your mind wanders, and instead of listening to your opposer, you think about your next statement or next question. All it takes is a moment's inattention to miss a switch. When it does happen, something unfortunate takes place: You get that feeling of bewilderment and you assume it is you, and not your opposer. In other words, when Our Hero gets confused he should immediately say, "Where did that come from?" or "Why did you bring that up?" Instead he pretends he *knows* why the conversation has taken this turn and tries to hide his confusion by pretending he follows the argument. Sound familiar?

Most arguers do not have the confidence to suppose that the other person has made a mistake or committed a

---

Toronto Star, 10 February 1989.
†*Toronto Star*, 3 February 1989.

fallacy when it's so much easier to blame themselves: "There I go again, too stupid to know what's happening, too thick to follow the argument. Well, he's pretty bright, so I suppose he knows what he's talking about." Like hell! All you do with this attitude is compound a felony. First you forget to listen; then, when you come back and are confused you assume it is you, not your opposer, who is at fault.

You can even do that when you *are* listening. Everything is going fine and then—POW!—confusion. At that moment most of you assume you have missed something your partner said, but instead of saying, "Wait, I must have missed something," you pretend to understand every word and move. This is always bad. If the confusion is not caused by a mistake, then you owe it to your respondent to try to follow his argument. If the confusion is caused by a shifty maneuver, you owe it to yourself to stop and ask. In either case, whether the bewilderment is your fault or your opposer's, you should look for the cause.

Trust your instincts.
If you are confused there must be
a reason. Check it out!

Another example of change of subject, which should help illustrate why you have to stay on your toes, is an argument about the role of myth in history. Should history as taught to school children describe the truth? Or should the rough edges and nastiness—as, for example, cases of government corruption—be excluded or edited?

OUR HERO: It's important that children grow up with a sense of reality. Teaching them that our country has never done wrong is a mistake. It gives them too strong a faith in leaders.

JOSH: Well now, they're only children. You don't want to scare them.

OUR HERO: It's not necessary to lay out every dirty fact. But presenting events as if there were no bad guys is too much. For one thing, it's contradicted by the daily newspapers. We're better off giving them the truth.

JOSH: And what, pray tell, is *that*? Who knows what really happened in any situation? What is truth in history? You can never be sure that any description of an historical event is really complete.

OUR HERO: [*Not falling for the bait.*] Sure, it's difficult to determine absolute truth in history, or anywhere, for that matter. But that's not what we're talking about. There are obvious things left out, incidents not related, particularly when it comes to leaders making shady deals. I'm not talking about absolute Truth, that would be silly, as you of course know. What I am talking about is making the stories less like fairy tales.

This is a good example of pulling an opposer back to the subject. Our Hero sealed that return with the comment that Josh, *of course*, knows that absolute truth is not the issue. Now, instead of getting off on whether history can ever be *the* Truth, they are continuing with the discussion of myth in education.

Sometimes you may not want to be subtle about getting the subject back on track. It might be to your advantage to let a respondent know in no uncertain terms that you are aware of the subject change, that you know very well what is going on. You might be dealing with a constant subject-switcher, a real ground-changer—most of whom (unless they are politicians) commit their fallacies unintentionally. Not only do they ignore *your* arguments and replies, but they do not even listen to their *own*. Since they have no idea what they are saying, it is nothing at all for them to say something else—any time they are offered the least resistance, they change the subject. Arguing with such people can be infuriating. In these cases the subject should be brought back firmly and obviously.

Be firm and obvious
with an habitual subject-switcher.

When you want to make a point of returning to the original subject, first let your partner finish. After your opposer has stopped, say something like, "That's fine. But we were talking about _____, and I would like to continue." Or, "I'm sorry, but you've changed the subject. I don't want to talk about that. Let's finish the first argument." A bit of time may have to be spent explaining why the subjects are different, but that is usually not too difficult. Watch Our Hero try this technique:

OUR HERO: By no means should we re-institute a draft.

SOPHIE: Well, I'm not so sure.

OUR HERO: Having a large standing army is an invitation to use it. It creates hardship in a time when it is not necessary. And besides, moves should be made to appear unwarlike.

SOPHIE: But don't you think that people owe service to their country?

OUR HERO: Look, Sophie, that's not what we're talking about. That's another story entirely. What I want to know is, do you think a draft should be re-instituted?

SOPHIE: Well, I just don't think there's anything wrong with serving your country.

OUR HERO: Neither do I. But you're changing the subject. We're talking about one way of being *forced* to do it, not whether it's good or bad to ever serve your country in any way. Get back to the topic.

The difficulty is that some people never listen, and if they do not listen, you cannot really argue with them. You might point that out, but results cannot be guaranteed. Everyone knows someone like good old Uncle Harry who hasn't heard a word anyone's said for years.

The key to beating a change of subject is, first of all, to know that it has happened. If the thread of an argument is lost, stop and find out what is going on. The odds are it had nothing to do with you.

16

Everyone's Doin' It, Doin' It, Doin' It

"Belcho Beer is the best-selling beer in the entire country. Could all those people be wrong?" This form of advertising is familiar to us all. What does it mean? How much weight does it carry? Take a look at one way in which Belcho's claim, while true, might be misleading. Suppose there was a beer industry composed of ten competitors, each with a fairly even share of the market: Seven of them have exactly 10 percent of the total market, two have 9 percent, and one—you guessed it, Belcho—has 12 percent. So, the difference that licenses Belcho's claim is 2 percent. Hardly that dramatic, although of course Belcho's stockholders are glad. But should *you* be impressed?

There is no fallacy committed when a company tells you that theirs is the leading product. The fallacy occurs if that is all they tell you. Why should you buy something just because everyone else is? It is interesting information and might even make you stop to consider the product, but it is not enough. "Most popular" does not always mean "best." There are always many reasons why a brand is the leading product, usually having to do with their marketing and advertising strategy. An effective advertising campaign is much more important than quality. Other reasons contribute to popularity. Some products are very old and deeply embedded in the public mind. Other products are "first" because they have very few, sometimes poor, competitors—any product can be "first" if it is the only competitor. Suppose you have a shampoo you want to advertise as the "leading" shampoo. Well, you cannot do that unless it *is* the leading shampoo. But wait! It may *not* be the *leading* shampoo, but it might be the *leading medicated* shampoo. And, if that isn't enough, the *leading medicated natural* shampoo.

Popularity alone is not enough.

What is important is *why* something is popular. The fallacy of **popularity** occurs when popularity is taken as the most important fact. (It also has a fancier name that can be used to impress opponents: *argumentum ad populum*, which means "argument to the people."

Factors contributing to popularity may be irrelevant in many cases. The very opposite view—that the most popular items are disappointing—also makes sense. After all, for a product to sell very widely it must appeal to a very broad segment of the population. One way to do this is to make a very excellent product, but another way is to make a very bland product—such as Belcho. (It should not surprise you that Belcho Beer indeed lacks character.)

Price is another factor important to popularity. Is the best-selling wine really the best *wine*? What about the best-selling washing machine or dishwasher? Is it also the best, or is there a more expensive one that will provide better service in the long run?

The fallacy of popularity takes other forms as well. One of them is illustrated in the following dialogue:

MATT: I really didn't expect the election to turn out that way.

LAUREN: Well, it sure didn't fool me.

MATT: How could you possibly have expected that? I thought Smith was a shoo-in.

LAUREN: Jones was the underdog. Everyone knows an underdog will wait and come from behind, just like Jones did. Anyone giving careful analysis could see that the underdog effect would work.

Lauren's last response to Matt employs two uses of the fallacy of popularity. The first is use of the expression "Everyone knows." Other familiar forms are "We all know," "It's common knowledge that . . . ," and "You are, of course, aware, as we all are, that. . . ." These are hard phrases to beat when everyone wants to be "in the know." Since you do not want to appear ignorant or stupid, you agree to almost anything rather than admit ignorance. Lauren seals up the fallacy very tightly the second time: "Anyone giving careful analysis. . . ." This expression has close relatives in "Anyone giving a moment's thought" or "Anyone who knows what's happening." At this point, to disagree with Lauren is like saying, "I did not give a careful analysis."

Here is another example of the fallacy of popularity:

OUR HERO: Choosing a car is difficult. It looks to me like a Ford is somewhat better made than a Chevy.

DIDI: Nonsense! Anyone who knows their cars would tell you that a Chevrolet is better than a Ford.

OUR HERO: Well, I guess I don't know cars because I just don't see it that way. Why does everyone think Chevrolet is better?

Didi is now on the spot, and must put up or shut up. If she thinks everyone knows, then she must know—and, by the Principle of Rationality, she must have reasons. If not, she will look foolish and lose credibility as well.

If your opposer says "Everyone knows . . . "
—and you don't know—
then your opposer is wrong.

We are our own evidence. "Everyone," according to our learned opponent, "knows that Smith is in the pocket of big business." But if *you* do not know it, if *you* do not have good reasons for believing it, then *you* have disproved your opposer's claim: You, after all, are part of Everyone.

It is difficult to respond to the popularity fallacy in the correct way. Remembering one thing might help: Not only is it a fallacy, but your opposer's statements are very often just plain false. Rarely does *everyone* know something terribly interesting. Very few do the necessary work to find out.

Usually people simply repeat what some opposer told *them* that everyone knows. This is called rumor, *not* fact; a *rumor* is something that should be checked, not believed. The popularity fallacy does not depend on your ignorance for its success, but on your fear of *seeming* ignorant. Not attacking the fallacy lets your opposer know that you are not only ignorant but gullible, so you are better off attacking.

*Never let the fear of
looking dumb make you argue poorly.
You're no dumber than anyone else.*

Another variant of the fallacy of popularity is found in the mistake called *provincialism*: assuming that what is close and familiar is better. When, for example, you know your city or country, it is easy to assume that *your* city or country is better than any other. Such assumptions usually are false. It is just easier to think that your country or religion or lifestyle is best; it feels good to believe that you are superior or free from errors and faults that other people have. This mistake or assumption often leads to a belief that your country can do no wrong, or your religion is the only real Truth.

This begins in school: If you teach children that their country has never done wrong, or that their religion is better than all the others, then, in later life, when faced with a foreign religion, a strange lifestyle, or the possibility that their country has committed an immoral act they will be totally unprepared to deal with it. They will find it much easier to believe what they are familiar with than what is strange and different.

A similar situation, common in race relations, is believing that *my* race is tolerant, understanding, kind, and generous; *they*, on the other hand, are pushy, intolerant, nasty, and selfish. The psychological foundations of prejudice are complicated and not at all clear, but the role that prejudice plays in argument is simple: Believe whatever supports your own group. This fallacy extends far beyond argument to a way of perceiving the world: Many people refuse to listen to or hear anything that threatens the foundation of their beliefs. One of these threats comes from a demand for equality from other races and nations. If you have reasons for not agreeing, fine and well; but it is your responsibility to acknowledge those reasons and to let them be known. The beauty of argument is that is knows no favorites. The same rules apply to all the participants.

17

Well, If He Said So . . .

It is impossible to know everything. No matter how much you read and discuss, you cannot become expert in every field. Once plumbing is conquered, biology remains. If theoretical physics is under control, then auto mechanics is baffling. There are just too many areas of expertise.

Normally this is not a hardship, because no one wants to know everything. But there are times when information not known to you is important when having an argument or making a decision. In these situations you generally call on an expert. The expert may not be a famous scientist or movie star, but simply the local auto mechanic, or your family doctor. Sometimes the expert is a friend "in the business" or an acquaintance who knows something or someone.

Suppose you are thinking about buying a new stereo system. You might well talk to salespeople or friends who are enthusiasts. For your purposes in this discussion, each of these people can be considered an expert.

> *An expert is*
> *anyone who knows more than you do*
> *when you want to know it.*

So, your neighbor with the $3500 stereo—who reads four hi-fi magazines a month and talks freely about tweeters, woofers, and wattage—is an expert, as is the audio engineer married to cousin Kathy.

The problem in dealing with experts is the *very* reason *for* dealing with them: They know more than you do. But it is all too easy to be misled by an expert. The neighbor with the $3,500 setup may be of little help if you are planning to spend a total of only $800. Yet, expert advice is essential: It would be foolish to spend even $800 on stereo equipment without seeking information from those who know.

Often situations requiring experts are both complicated and controversial. A great deal of the debate on the safety of video display terminals, for example, involves conflicting expert testimony. In recent times, more than ever before, the expert is being challenged both by other experts and by the public. The popularity of issues such as environmental control, space exploration, and even corporate expansion and monopoly have led to pitched battles—in public—between experts on all sides.

The misuse of experts is both frequent and common. Incorrect appeals to authority form the basis of the fallacy of **authority** or *argumentum ad verecundiam*. Fallacious appeals to authority occur often because you need more information than any one person can manage. But, the difficulties posed by this need for experts are easily overcome. The first and most vital step is the elimination of your awe of experts. For some reason perfectly capable, intelligent people lose all perspective when dealing with someone who knows something they do not.

Remember: You are an expert, too, and you know how little you know.

Any of us is capable of giving reasonable advice on some subject or other. It may have to do with a job, a hobby or pastime, but there is surely at least one small area in which each of us is an expert and might be asked for or offer advice.

At the same time you know perfectly well that the advice you offer will be subject to prejudices, training, needs, and experience. Suppose, for example, that Jacob is a stereo buff. He may well be asked by a friend for advice on purchasing some equipment. But, because he is familiar with the field, he is also aware of the complications. Jacob knows, for example, that his friend should spend his money one way if he generally listens to classical music and another way if he is a rock fan. This is obvious. But when *you* want advice from someone else, all this is forgotten. Too often anything they say will be taken as the "gospel truth"—after all, they know what they are talking about. If *you* apply the same caution to other experts that you apply to yourself you'll be off to a good start.

One of the most frequent mistakes involving experts occurs when they are used in the wrong field. The most obvious example of this sort of fallacy is the celebrity performer who recommends a product. Ray Charles might very well be worth listening to on the merits of musical instruments, and I would not at all mind his advice on buying stereo equipment, but is he an expert on soft drinks? I have seen a photograph of a Dallas Cowboy quarterback attached to promotional material for heavy tractors. There is no indication at all that even the best quarterback is prepared to choose intelligently among heavy tractors.

> *No one is simply an expert—*
> *an expert must be an expert*
> *in something.*

The expert you are seeking or the one being used against you in an argument must be from the right field. Athletes selling cars and tractors are the most blatant, but others are harder to identify. A famous example involved Dr. Benjamin Spock during the height of the anti–Vietnam war movement. Spock, an expert in child care, was all of a sudden being taken to be an authority on foreign affairs. There is, of course, absolutely no reason why Dr. Spock should not have spoken out as he did. He had every right to do so; indeed he claimed that he had an obligation to do so. But what *was* wrong was that Spock's fame or achievements as a pediatrician somehow lent greater authority or force to his opinions. Spock's arguments were not being weighed on their own merits, but on his reputation as a pediatrician.

In recent years it has seemed almost impossible to get elected without an entire supporting cast from Hollywood. We should not care who Jane Fonda, Madonna, Tom Cruise, or any other star is voting for—and that is no reflection on their intelligence or their talent. They are simply *not* experts, and if they are treated as such, then the fallacy of appeal to authority is committed.

*If the expert appealed to
is not appropriate,
then a fallacy is committed.*

One of the real difficulties with experts is that it is very hard to identify just what they are expert in. If you are arguing with a biologist, you should not expect him to know everything about *every* branch of biology. And really a good auto mechanic, in fact, should refer you to a specialist when it comes to transmission problems. So, how careful do you have to be? The answer depends on how technical and narrow is the information you want. If it is a general question in biology, there is no need to get a specialist. But if the argument is about a very fine point, perhaps the effect of a chemical on a fish or animal, then a high degree of specialization is required. The way to determine if the expert is indeed a specialist is to ask. Notice in the following dialogue how Our Hero both recognizes and exposes a misuse of authority.

JOSH: That substance in the water should not have the effect on the adrenal gland that Professor Martin describes.

OUR HERO: Is endocrinology the field in which you do your work?

JOSH: No, not exactly. I'm in a closely-related field.

OUR HERO: Have you ever written anything or lectured on endocrinology?

JOSH: No. But it forms a part of the regular program of study for any biologist.

OUR HERO: I see, so you really don't know any more about it than any other biologist. So, how can you disagree with Professor Martin, an endocrinologist?

The authority has been put in his place: He is not a specialist in the field. All too often we are impressed by scientists because they are scientists, not because they know what they are talking about. Using an expert from the wrong area is another instance of the fallacy of authority or *argumentum ad verecundiam*.

Authorities can appear impressive even to you when their colleagues might not be moved. An expert with a Ph.D. in economics, a list of credentials, and a great private fortune, for example, might recommend investing heavily in the commodities market, when most other financial advisers would not. You may not know if you are being given an unusual opinion or a standard response. Assuming that other authorities would agree with this expert might be a mistake.

> *Is the authority giving you*
> *generally accepted facts*
> *or an unusual personal opinion?*
> *Find out.*

Here is how the economics problem might be handled.

OUR HERO: I don't know. The commodities market is supposed to be very tricky and dangerous. Are you sure about this recommendation?

LAUREN: Certainly. That is the very best place, right now, to make money.

OUR HERO: I'm really surprised. Would most financial consultants agree with this advice?

LAUREN: The smart ones would.

OUR HERO: But would most of them?

LAUREN: No, most wouldn't. They try to scare people out of the commodities market for no good reason.

Our Hero should be happy that Lauren is a maverick offering a controversial opinion rather than mainstream advice. This does not mean the expert is wrong, just that caution should be used. After all, the whole problem in consulting authorities is that you often have to accept their word for something. And if their word is not generally agreed upon, the value of their advice is diminished.

Other ways of checking out the experts include examining their track records and investigating what other beliefs they hold. These areas should especially be checked when using an expert publicly. You can be embarrassed when offering an expert's agreement if your opposer replies, "Oh, yes. I've heard of him. He's the guy who thinks cats and dogs should be made to wear diapers in public." Even if your man is the very best in his field, his credibility has been undermined. Another danger is that the authority you have cited may be in the habit of making rash predictions—the expert may have a bad case of news conference-itis, a disease sometimes plaguing the scientific establishment. Not quite as embarrassing as your expert who wore diapers, but it will not help the cause if the expert scientist is remembered as having predicted the ozone layer would completely vanish by 1993.

Know your experts:
Do they hold embarrassing beliefs?
Do they make rash predictions?

We must all deal with authorities—from experts who understand complicated issues and burning questions right down to your neighborhood auto mechanic and computer salesperson. Even dealing with these local experts can be a chilling experience for many people. Computer experts often seem to revel in the combination of their special knowledge and our ignorance. It seems that as fast as your technical competence about computers increases through valiant attempts to learn from magazines and manuals, so do the computers themselves become more and more complicated. Many males, bearing the sexist cross of being "supposed to know," have purchased manuals entitled "Understanding Your Computer: A Guide for Women," or one of those books designed for the technologically impaired.

There is nothing worse to some males than having to admit ignorance about machines. This is, sadly, becoming common among females as well: Knowledge about the computer is now one among many symbols of competence. The computer salesperson knows you are reluctant to admit ignorance, and can easily take advantage of you. But the problem is still there—most of us are abysmally ignorant about the stupid machines.

There is, however, a solution to the difficulties of dealing with computer consultants, and it applies to auto mechanics, scientists, plumbers, plasterers, and doctors as well: You must learn to feel pride in your ignorance. After all, you might be an accountant, or stock clerk, or homemaker, or whatever: It is not your job to know about RAM or megabytes, so why should you? Your very reason for going to an expert is because it is her job. So, the first half of the solution is to freely admit, even flaunt, your ignorance. This prevents premature agreement.

Never agree with an expert
unless you really do know
what she is talking about—
no matter how stupid you feel.

A true expert is familiar with her work—so familiar that she should be able to explain it to anybody, even if completely ignorant about the subject. You must demand explanations from local experts until you really do understand. They may not like it. (I am convinced the service manager of my local auto dealership has homicidal fantasies about me, because I cannot tolerate the thought of paying all that money without knowing why.) But persist doggedly with your questions until you really do understand what is going on. Do not succumb to the temptation to say, "Oh. If the frammis is frozen you've got to replace the geegaw." Why pretend when you don't even know a frammis from a geegaw?

Remember what I pointed out at the beginning of this chapter: You are an expert. Although it is only reasonable that there are things you do not know, it is also reasonable (and this is truly liberating) that there are things you do not *want* to know. Remember, too, in dealing with an expert, ignorance can be your most important weapon. The key to dealing with experts is to demand an explanation: An expert should be able to explain to anyone. Any expert unwilling to explain should be viewed with suspicion. Any expert refusing to explain is violating the Principle of Rationality and should be avoided.

18

The Refuge of Scoundrels

Arguing can be a long, tiring, involved business. Getting someone to agree, attempting to change someone's mind, can take a good deal of effort. Simple persuasion, on the other hand, when there is no concern for method, truth, honesty, or principle is another matter. When argument is forsaken in favor of manipulation, unscrupulous opposers can save considerable time and effort. Often people who are very sure of the truth of their positions (or the justness of their causes or the importance of their goals) will care only about results: In these cases a frequently used device is the **attack on the person**—most commonly known by its Latin tag, *argumentum ad hominem*.

Polly Politician is running for office again and is insecure about this election. She knows she is the better candidate and therefore has a right to use whatever means necessary to defeat her foe. Here is a part of her speech to an audience of veterans. Counting on the fact that she's addressing a generally conservative group and is receiving newspaper attention, she freely smears her opponent:

> POLLY: I am running for office—not for myself, not for glory, not for my party. I will accept great burdens for myself and my family in taking this job. Why then shall I do it? I do it for one reason only: my country! [*Applause.*] Does my country need me? Of course not. Whom am I? Just a citizen and voter like you. I am just someone with a deep devotion to this great land and the principles on which it stands. Why then do I run? The answer is simple: There are those who would undo all the great things, all the great principles, fought for by all the great patriots who have lived and died for this country throughout its glorious history. [*Applause.*] I speak of those who are not devoted to the family, to freedom, but who are self-serving and confused. I speak of those who would lead us in their confusion into the hands of the devil, of our enemies. Is my opponent a womanizer? A devil worshipper? A pederast? I do not know. But I don't care about labels. Just look at his policies: Where do his sympathies lie? I ask you, who can you trust?

Polly can go on indefinitely. She has not directly called her opponent a pervert, but simply created a strong association. She is name-calling. She has not dealt at all with her opponent's statements, issues, or policies. This nasty and underhanded form of attack was used by Senator Joseph

McCarthy during the witchhunts for communists in the 1950s. It is a very powerful device before a sympathetic audience, and really very simple: It is almost impossible to prove that you are *not* something.

Imagine that someone has accused Liz of being dishonest and sneaky. How would Liz go about proving that person wrong? It may be impossible. She may call witnesses from among friends, relatives, and acquaintances, but they may be dismissed since they all like her and can hardly be expected to say anything else. The only other thing Liz might do is point up times when she did particularly honest things. But this is all just evidence showing how sneaky she is: Real sneaks are never discovered, they always *appear to be* honest and trustworthy. This sort of smear tactic is hard to beat.

There are a number of different attitudes concerning the correct response to this sort of attack. One is to ignore it. But are such smears ever really ignored? Another response is to say it does not deserve the dignity of a reply. But in doing so one has replied, saying implicitly that the charge is nonsense. A good reply might be, "These tactics are used from time to time in every campaign. Some people will stoop to anything, and I think *that* is the most interesting point to arise from Polly's statements. I leave it to the voters to decide if they want me or someone who uses smear tactics and name-calling." This, however, is often traditionally labeled "refusing to reply." Another possible response makes use of humor: "Sure, I know that Polly called me a leftwinger. She'd probably label Lincoln a leftwinger for freeing the slaves! She's so far to the right she has to look backwards just to make a left turn."

All these replies fail if the context is not public. Someone accused at work, for example, will likely never get a chance to reply in any way at all. So, in these situations, the best reaction all around is to point up the evil as it is happening. "What is your evidence for saying Liz is a sneak and a gossip? Come on, what gives?" By reacting in this way you have a reasonable hope that you will be saved when it is your turn.

If someone attacks a person's character,
insist that he put up or shut up.

There are other forms of name-calling also common but not quite as out-and-out vicious. Here the opposer describes those who disagree in an unfavorable way. Usually they are dismissed as "naysayers" or "dissidents" or "a small minority of unsatisfied diehards." What these phrases mean is that the individuals disagree, which is perfectly accurate. The implication, however, is that nothing would satisfy these people. One of the most famous of all such labels harks back to the much-quoted dismissal of anti-Vietnam war protesters used by Spiro Agnew, Vice President under Richard Nixon. Agnew labeled those who disagreed with the war effort as "an effete corps of impudent snobs."

Let us watch Our Hero in a brief interchange with Polly:

OUR HERO: Tell me, Polly, what is your opinion of the charges leveled against the proposed atomic energy plant?

POLLY: Atomic energy is a cheap, safe, sure source of fuel.

OUR HERO: That's nice, Polly. But tell me about *your* reactions to the criticisms.

POLLY: These people are nothing but a small group of fanatics trying to undermine a vast, important project that will benefit many people and create 129 new jobs.

OUR HERO: OK. Just tell me one thing: Are the fanatics right?

POLLY: Of course not. They are just know-nothing do-gooders.

OUR HERO: But *why* are they wrong, Polly?

POLLY: You'll have to excuse me, but I have another appointment across town.

Our Hero has realized that the question is not how the dissidents are to be labeled, but how Polly is to respond to their arguments.

Even when the nasty names really apply to people, their arguments stand or fall on their own worth, not the worth of whoever offered the argument. According to newspaper reports a politician recently labeled a constituent a "ding-dong" because she'd written him a letter opposing a pay raise for legislators. The constituent might have replied very effectively with this: "I have been called a ding-dong. Well and fine. But what this ding-dong wants to know is how can these pay raises be justified."

Labels apply to people,
not to their arguments.

Another sort of attack addressing itself to the person and not the argument aims to discredit them because of who they are, or because of their circumstances. Dismissing an argument by prison guards just because they are prison guards constitutes a fallacy: It is just not a good enough reason.

During the Augusto Pinochet dictatorship in Chile (1973–1990), the Chilean ambassador to Canada responded to charges of torture there by calling those who gave testimony on the subject "political enemies of the Chilean government who have long been absent from the country." This attack is irrelevant since it is about their background and not their statements. (I have seen similar claims made by other ambassadors as well.)

These days an especially insidious form of *argumentum ad hominem* stalks the land. Individuals are accused of saying or doing things that are racist or sexist because they disagree with someone's position. Opposing a program or a position that is popular with some group, however, does not mean that you are against that group; opposing it means you are not satisfied with the *reasons* for the position or program. Attacking opposers because they disagree with *you*, rather than attacking the reasons for a claim, is an example of the fallacy.

---

*Disagreeing with the position of a group
does not mean you are against that group.*

Individuals' lifestyles are irrelevant to the truth or falsity of their claims. One interviewer, questioning the Reverend Jesse Jackson about the busing issue, raised a series of questions about Jackson's lifestyle: He was asked where he lived, the size of his car, the size of his house, and other personal questions. Jackson might live in a mansion or a one-room shack—it matters not at all to his argument. It might matter for other things, but not for determining the value of his position on school busing. Jackson unfortunately went on to address himself to these points rather than simply pointing out their irrelevance.

Our Hero will have a crack at dealing with an attack to the person:

> OUR HERO: Probably the stickiest argument against abortion is the one about the sanctity of life. I don't know how to dismiss that one at all.
>
> ANNE-LISE: Oh, you mean the Catholic argument.
>
> OUR HERO: Yes, that one.
>
> ANNE-LISE: Well, only Catholics hold that position, and they're *all* against abortion.
>
> OUR HERO: So?
>
> ANNE-LISE: Well, come on, the only reason they put forward an argument like that is because they're against abortion in the first place. If they weren't against abortion, they would never say that.
>
> OUR HERO: Sure, Anne-lise, but it's still an argument. I have no idea, really, whether anyone believes it—but that just doesn't matter. What we need is a counter-argument.

Our Hero has stopped Anne-lise from dismissing the argument simply because it is presented by Catholics. They may well be pushing the position *because* they are Catholics—Anne-lise may be right—but it is still necessary to eliminate the argument, rather than the person or the group.

The most common example of *argumentum ad hominem* is the use of an expression like, "Well, what would you expect her to say? After all, she's . . . ," followed by the explanation of her interest in the case. A train conductor arguing for improvements in rail service, a general arguing for more defense funds, an ecologist warning about future shortages, a professor extolling the virtues of higher education—to all of these it is easy to reply with a dismissal since you "know what they think." And it might even be true that the arguments these people give *is* exactly what you would expect them to say. But so what? Now that they have said it, what will you reply?

A person's background may explain
why they give an argument,
but it will not be
grounds for dismissing it.

One difficulty with the attack to the person is that in some situations a person's background and character *are* important. For example, when someone is presented as an expert or authority, certain aspects of his or her background become relevant. An authority's track record, history, and standing within a particular community of experts may be relevant in determining his or her reliability. And, speaking of testimony, information about a person's character and background may be relevant in a court of law. If someone giving testimony has a reputation as a liar or perjurer, you can be sure that a lawyer will want the jury to know about this witness's history. There is, though, an obvious difficulty captured in the story of the boy who cried wolf: Someone may well have a reputation for lying and yet be telling the truth in this instance. For this reason it is imperative that an attack on the person or even character investigation be limited to those times when it is absolutely essential.

You may have heard people dispute a claim by saying something like, "That's no good. It is just an *ad hominem.*" This error is a form of an even more general move, traditionally called the *genetic fallacy* (from the term "genesis"), and it involves confusing the truth or falsity of an argument with its origins. The genetic fallacy occurs when governments buy from certain firms for reasons other than the value of the product. If, for example, geographic location or economic factors are considered and the reasons for using this information are not given and defended, then the genetic fallacy is committed.

Another example of the genetic fallacy involves the *origin of ideas*. An idea or invention might be rejected (or accepted) just because it is Russian or Chinese or Islamic. Watch:

OUR HERO: Wouldn't it be great if all the government officials and bureaucrats had to spend time at physical jobs, and maybe even be required to go to government offices *incognito* to get forms or information? I think that would really make them nicer, more responsive to our problems.

JOSH: Oh, no you don't! I know where that comes from. That's the sort of nonsense that went on in China, isn't it?

OUR HERO: Yes. They had whole systems geared to keeping officials in touch with the problems of the ordinary people.

JOSH: Foo! I don't go for any of that commie stuff here. We have enough problems of our own without starting that sort of nonsense.

The best thing for Our Hero to do now is quit the argument. He might lie and say they are trying it out in England, but I hope that is beneath him.

When an argument is attacked for its source or its origins the fallacy of ad hominem *has been committed.*

A last, common form of the genetic fallacy is the *dismissal of ideas* that have previously gotten into trouble. Like children caught in the act, such ideas are condemned to a future marked with doubt and mistrust. Socialized medicine, guaranteed income, or whatever, may have flopped at one time in the past, but unless reasons are given for supposing it will *not* work now, a fallacy has been committed. You cannot know that an idea will not work if tried in a different place and in a different manner. Bottle- and can-recycling programs may thrive in one area and flop miserably in another, but the failures provide opportunities to learn for the next attempt—they do not necessarily mean the idea itself is wrong.

Name-calling, smearing, and dismissing arguments because of their source are all ways of avoiding the real issue. These tactics are common among those who do not wish to listen or consider. Beware: If a person's character, motives, or background is raised, demand to know why it is relevant to the argument.

19

The Straw-Man Argument

Shadow-boxing can provide a person with exercise, training, and a feeling of accomplishment. But there is a catch: When finished with the boxing drill, one cannot turn around and say, "Well, I sure beat him." After all, no one was beaten; it was all make-believe. There is a similar situation in argument. Sometimes an arguer will viciously, mercilessly, and dramatically destroy a position. The destruction is total and the position is in ruins. But, the arguer is "shadow-arguing": No one holds the attacked position. The arguer is fighting an imaginary foe, not just in the sense that no opposer was present, but also in the sense that no opposer could be found.

It frequently happens in arguments that a position is attacked when there is really no one there to defend it. Here is a quick vignette illustrating this situation:

LAUREN: What do you think of this teachers' strike?

MATT: I think they want to run the whole school system all by themselves, and that, as far as I am concerned, is crazy.

LAUREN: What do you mean?

MATT: There should be community involvement as well as teacher input. And there is no way the whole board of education should be thrown out just because teachers say so.

LAUREN: Well, I certainly wouldn't want to chuck out the board.

Lauren is now agreeing with Matt on Matt's version of the striking teachers' demands. It would be interesting to see if they would agree on the real demands. Did Matt really capture the sense of the demands? Do the teachers really want all decision-making power? Do they not want any other group, particularly the board or parents, to have a say? These are very radical, strong desires—in fact, they are suspiciously strong. Are there really any teachers who hold this view? And if so, are they a large enough group for their views to be labeled "the teachers' view"? There may be *some* teachers who hold the position described by Matt, but how many?

The fallacy of **straw man** is committed when a position is distorted. The position is made more radical or extreme than it really is, making it easier to attack. A student might have several interesting arguments for the abolition of grades in a university. Rather than dealing with these arguments, an opposer might portray the student's position as one that calls for eliminating any evaluation and giving out degrees just for the asking. This is a much easier position to attack. Another example involves abortion debates: By characterizing the pro-abortion position as far more radical than it is, an opponent of abortion is able to point out many awful consequences of liberalizing abortion. If the opposition describes the position as not having a time limit after which abortions may not be performed, the pictures and verbal descriptions of late-term abortions will provide endless hours of emotional ammunition. If the position were more accurately portrayed, this would not happen.

> *When given a radical position,*
> *ask yourself:*
> *Does anyone really hold this view?*

Not all instances of the straw-man fallacy are intentional. Sometimes people really do misunderstand a position, or they may have been given wrong information. Nonetheless, the distortion is still there. What complicates matters even more is that the media, for instance, always give more play to the most radical fringe of any group.

> *Given any position,*
> *—no matter how crazy or extreme—*
> *you can always find someone who holds it.*

People on the radical fringe of a group, just because they are so outrageous, make for more interesting listening and reading than the moderate members of a group. Consequently, it is the radical fringe we hear about. A well-known example is the women's rights movement, back in the early 1970s: The vast majority of women were essentially moderate, but the media reported almost exclusively on those elements of the movement that were sure to get the strongest reaction.

In the following dialogue Our Hero will smell a rat and try to get more information.

> JOSH: You know, I think these environmental groups are crazy.
>
> OUR HERO: Why crazy?
>
> JOSH: Well, if they had their way, we'd shut down every factory . . . boom, just like that!
>
> OUR HERO: Really?
>
> JOSH: Really. And the economy would come to a grinding halt—massive unemployment, enormous dislocation, starvation and anarchy. Just to save some trees.
>
> OUR HERO: Well, that certainly does seem like a high price to pay. Are you sure that's the position?
>
> JOSH: You bet it is. But they're fanatics, so what can you expect?
>
> OUR HERO: Well, Josh, maybe some extremists would hold that position, but I can't believe many do. There must be a lot in favor of cleaning up factories instead of closing them. Maybe we should do some research.

Our Hero was alerted by the following rule of thumb:

Always be suspicious of positions
that are too easy to attack:
They have very likely been distorted.

Distortion of your own position can be halted by interrupting with something like this: "That's a very interesting view. However, it has nothing to do with my position. Let me explain again."

In the next dialogue Sophie will try to saddle Our Hero with a radical position:

OUR HERO: There is too much money spent on defense in this country.

SOPHIE: I suppose what we ought to do is just invite our enemies in for a picnic. Is that what you think?

OUR HERO: Don't be silly. I'm not against defense, I'm just questioning the amount spent.

SOPHIE: If we don't have a strong defense force, we'll be overrun. Would you want that?

OUR HERO: Look, Sophie, I don't know what you're getting so excited about. I don't want to eliminate the defense budget or throw out our defenses. All I'm suggesting is that too much is being spent. There probably is an incredible amount of waste.

SOPHIE: Too many people these days find it easy to attack things they don't know anything about. Defense is vital to survival. When you cut defense spending, you're cutting down our chances of survival. I think that's dangerous, unless you don't want us to survive.

OUR HERO: What nonsense, Sophie. You're distorting everything. Who said anything about not surviving? Don't put your words in my mouth!

Sophie seems to be fairly uninterested in Our Hero's argument. All she is trying to do is scare Our Hero. This is a common form of distortion: altering the position into one that is immensely unpopular or dangerous. If your opponent browbeats you, and you are not careful, you can succumb to the fear and abandon your position. Browbeating is not uncommon in situations where loyalty or patriotism may *seem* to be an issue; but in most cases it is only the *distortion* that makes patriotism relevant.

The only defense against distortion is observance of Super-Rule II: If you are always listening, you will hear any distortions and object to them. Please remember that you must listen to your *own* arguments as well as to your respondent's. In this way you will be aware of any differences between your version and your opposer's. The ability to know your position is crucial: You cannot reasonably expect to win arguments if you are defending distortions.

20

The Slippery Slope

In chapter 1 Our Hero encountered an uncooperative motor vehicle clerk. The clerk feared that if she reached over for the form Our Hero wanted, in no time at all she would be running about all over the place fetching this and that for everyone—to the insurance department in the next room to get insurance forms, to the certification office upstairs to get certification forms, and on and on endlessly. And the clerk was quite right in not wanting to carry this burden. After all, she is paid a modest wage for standing behind a window and giving out one sort of form. Yet, her argument contained a fallacy: She need not go to any of those other places at all; she need not move off her seat at all; all she need do is reach over for the requested form. The clerk's argument was that if she fulfilled Our Hero's request, she would then have to perform those other duties. This is where the fallacy lies.

The same reasons do not apply to getting a form upstairs as apply to reaching over to the next window. As soon as the situation changes, the reasons change. The Principle of Similar Cases states that situations treated differently must be different, and there is a considerable difference in time, energy, and impact on those waiting if the clerk goes away from her post. So there is no good reason to accept her argument—as the situation changes, so will the reasons.

*You will slide down the slippery slope
unless you remember that
different statements need different reasons.*

The clerk viewed the situation as if she were on top of a steep **slippery slope**: If she takes just one step onto the slope, she will slide down and not be able to stop herself. Most situations are not at all like slippery slopes, but more like staircases: At each step you can stop and decide if you should go on by examining the next step down. Sometimes the distance between two steps is so small that you may fail to see the difference. For example, when purchasing a new car, the salesman, making a pitch for the options, will frequently point out that you have already decided to spend $15,500 and all he is talking about is $1,000 for air-conditioning. After all, if you are already spending such a large sum how much more will the small amount increase it? This is fine except that you do have to pay the $1,000—or more if you keep falling prey to this sort of reasoning.

Sometimes slopes really are slippery, and it becomes impossible to draw a line between two steps on the slope. This occurs in the arguments concerning abortion because it is important to know when a fetus becomes a person. Simply put, if a fetus is a person it has rights—in particular, the right *not* to be killed. Witness part of a debate on abortion between Our Hero and Didi:

> DIDI: I don't see what the fuss is about. Sure, a baby just before it's born is a person, but not at, say, six weeks. How can you compare the two?
>
> OUR HERO: Well, they certainly are different. But let me ask you this: You say that just before birth, let's say at eight months, a fetus is a person?
>
> DIDI: That's right. I confess that the few moments before birth can't make the difference between a person and a nonperson.
>
> OUR HERO: Well, then, what about seven months and 30 days? If a fetus is a person at eight months, what about the day before? Is a fetus not a person the day before?
>
> DIDI: No, it's not.
>
> OUR HERO: What is the difference?
>
> DIDI: I don't know. I suppose it must be a person at seven months and 30 days.
>
> OUR HERO: What about a week before that? Does something happen in that week to make it a person?
>
> DIDI: I don't know. No!
>
> OUR HERO: You see, of course, that we can just keep going back and back. You must find a relevant difference between two days, and you can't.

Our Hero has made a good point. Among the many arguments in the abortion debate, this is one of the most difficult.

The crucial question in judging the slipperiness of a slope is whether the several steps on it are identical. Our Hero here encounters an auto mechanic reluctant to take a moment to fix his car. Notice how Our Hero determines that the mechanic has a good case.

> OUR HERO: Excuse me, but I'm having a bit of trouble.
>
> JOSH: OK, hang on a moment. [*After a bit Josh looks at Our Hero's ailing car and informs him it just needs an adjustment to the carburetor, a 20-minute task.*]
>
> OUR HERO: In that case, could you please do it while I wait? It would be a great convenience for me.
>
> JOSH: I'm sorry. There are other cars that have been here all day. You'll have to wait your turn. I might not be able to get to it until tomorrow morning.
>
> OUR HERO: But you said it would only take 20 minutes. Why can't you just do it right away?
>
> JOSH: I can't work like that. It's first come, first served. If I let you get ahead, everyone will want to.
>
> OUR HERO: But how many people have problems that take only 20 minutes?
>
> JOSH: Quite a few. If I stop to do all of them, I'll never get the bigger jobs done. You can leave it here or bring it back in the morning—take your pick.

Our Hero determined that Josh was not just being arbitrary, but was faced with a potential flood of delays. Being a fair arguer and convinced that further discussion would be a waste of time, he left. (One way of winning an argument is by knowing when you can save time and just leave.)

The key to winning arguments involving slippery slopes is adherence to the Principle of Similar Cases: Is each of the steps exactly the same?

There are always two questions
to be asked about a slippery slope:
1. Is the slope truly slippery?
2. Should the first step be taken?

If each of the steps is just like the previous one, the next question is: Should the first step be taken? If the slope is slippery and the first step must be taken, there is nothing you can do but enjoy the slide and then come at the problem from another direction. If the first step can be avoided, however, then you should not take it to begin with. In all cases, always reserve judgment on whether the slope is indeed slippery. In this next example Our Hero grants an assumption about slipperiness only to remind Matt later on that it was a tentative assumption.

MATT: If a guaranteed minimum income is instituted, it will mean the end of this country as we know it.

OUR HERO: How?

MATT: Well, the greatness of this country stems from the industriousness of its people. The guaranteed minimum income will destroy that by eliminating incentive. That, in turn, will put more people on the dole, which will further weaken the workforce and increase the burden on the taxpayer. As the burden on working taxpayers increases, they will become more and more discouraged until they finally quit and join the others on the dole. That's how.

OUR HERO: Let's suppose for the moment your scenario is right. Does that still provide a reason *not* to have a guaranteed minimum income?

MATT: Well, I for one think those are pretty horrible results.

OUR HERO: I suppose, if we couldn't get people to work at all, things would be pretty bad.

MATT: Right. It would be pretty awful, wouldn't it?

OUR HERO: It would. But remember, I granted you the whole sequence of events leading to disaster. In fact, I don't think that's what would happen—I don't think the guarantee would destroy incentive. That alone is enough to stop your slippery slope.

The argument will now continue on the new subject: Will the guaranteed minimum income destroy incentive? If this is proven by Matt, he wins; he has already shown that, if his slope is indeed slippery, the end follows. Now they must argue about that first step.

The above example provides another reason why listening is important. Frequently, you will be asked to grant an assumption or imagine something is true when you do not really believe it is. This is very common in arguments, but if you are listening you will remember what your partner's claim rests on and can take it back when necessary.

Always keep track
of what assumptions you have granted
for the sake of argument—
you may want to take one of them back.

21

Haste Makes Waste

This section deals with three fallacies, all centered on the same theme: jumping to conclusions. The three fallacies—*doubtful evidence, false cause,* and *hasty generalization*—all involve moving too quickly from reason to conclusion.

A statement needs more than reasons for acceptance— it needs good reasons.

Doubtful evidence, a fallacy that is both simple and difficult to avoid involves the use of false or unreasonable evidence. The only real checks against it are investigation and intuition. It often is unrealistic if not impossible to verify statements because the work or information required may be beyond your resources.

An excellent instance of doubtful evidence was provided by Ronald Reagan when he described an infamous Chicago "welfare chiseler." The welfare cheat was alleged by Reagan to be earning over $150,000 in tax-free cash, a figure large enough to make any audience of taxpayers see red. A reporter wondered how the chiseler could get away with all this, so he decided to investigate. (This of course was the reporter's job; most of us could not take the time to investigate, and if we did we would not know how to go about it.) It turned out that the charges laid against the woman alleged fraud of only $8,000, not $150,000. And, while Reagan had claimed she had 80 aliases, the state charged her with using only four. How could you have known this? How could you have suspected that the information was being exaggerated? There is no real way. The only method available is a defensive attitude.

Believe nothing.

The only way to keep from believing false statements is not to believe any statements. By believing nothing you are protecting yourself. When reading a report in the papers a nonbeliever will always wonder what is *really* happening. Most reports in the media are biased in one way or another, so the only reasonable approach is to acquire as much information as possible and sift through it for the common elements and reasonable kernels. These can then be tentatively held for verification, almost believed, or treated as if they were believed—but you should never be surprised when they turn out false. If you stubbornly refuse to really believe anything, you can never go wrong, and those things that you do eventually come to believe stand a better chance of being true. There are many people who really do believe things just because they are in the papers, said by someone famous, or told to them by a supposedly informed source. It is not safe to believe so much.

What is written in newspapers may be connected casually to the truth, may be part of the story, or may be wholly fabricated. What the paper says one day may be retracted the next day; or the denial of whatever charges are made may be buried deep in the body of the article, where most readers never wander. Here's a good example: In a newspaper article a while ago a member of the Canadian Parliament was accused of irregularity in election financing; he had received a discount on room rates without declaring it as a donation. At the time there was a lot of concern about such issues. The charge was serious and was placed on the first page. Several days later an article appeared on page three explaining that the politician in question had only used the rooms during the day for resting and changing, and that was why the rate was lower—as it would be for anyone. How many people read the original charges on page one, and how many saw the small item on page three?

One of my favorites was on the front page of the *Toronto Star* quite some time ago. The following headline appeared in large type:

ANGOLAN FEMALE FIRING SQUAD
SHOOTS 17 CUBANS FOR RAPE*

Toronto Star, 11 March 1976.

The first three paragraphs fill in this headline with details that sound like a lead-in from a sensationalistic, true-confessions tabloid. The women were supposed to have identified and shot the Cubans. However, if you read on as far as the fourth paragraph—one paragraph further than most readers go—you learn that the Angolan government has denied the report "with utmost force." What actually happened? We will never know for sure, and certainly never from reading the paper.

If you want to win arguments, you must learn to be a Doubting Thomas. Skeptics—that is, doubters—always have a better chance since they have less to defend. The more you have to defend, the more there is open to attack. It's as simple as that. The only cost to being a skeptic is no longer having positions on everything. Most of us have views on just about every subject under the sun; a skeptic, however, will frequently answer "I'm not sure" when asked for an opinion. More is learned by hearing others' beliefs on abortion, education, capital punishment, sex, religion, and politics. It is true that there are times when you must make decisions. You have to vote, support issues and so on; at these times you can sit back, reflect on all the arguments, and hope you decide wisely.

Skeptics believe less,
and so have to defend less.

The fallacy of *false cause* is similar to doubtful evidence. Reasonable explanations are given, and they *could* be true, but there is just no reason to think they *are* true.

*Don't think that,
because one thing might be
a cause of another,
that it is.*

Suppose that someone states that the cause of poverty is lack of education. This has a certain appeal to it, a certain air of reasonableness, but few things, let alone social problems, have just one cause. Another cause of poverty is lack of jobs; still others include poor housing, prejudice, and poor nutrition. Someone else might say just the opposite, that a lack of education is caused by poverty—after all, the poor cannot afford to stay in school and have to go to work at an early age.

The key to pinpointing a false cause is coming up with another reasonable cause that is different from the first. Pointing out that it may not be lack of education but prejudice that leads to poverty confuses things; now there are two equally reasonable explanations. When you do that, your partner may back off and say that perhaps they are *both* causes. On the other hand your opposer may choose to defend his or her original reason. In that case, she must provide reasons for claiming that one cause and not the other is the crucial or real one.

*An explanation is a false cause fallacy
if other explanations are easily found.*

Some time ago someone pointed out that there had been an increase in the incidence of heart disease. At the same time North American consumption of animal fat dropped by 11 percent while consumption of vegetable fat increased by 75 percent. The spokesman pointed out that perhaps the cause of the increase in heart disease was the increased consumption of vegetable fats. This is a classic example of false cause: The simple correlation of two statistics—the decrease in animal fat consumption and the increase in heart disease—is far from sufficient as evidence for one's causing the other. (The spokesman, by the way, was speaking on behalf of the meat industry.)

Another example involving food comes from a bread producer. Preservatives are added to bread to keep it fresh longer; the cause of this, according to a bakery spokesman, is that people don't want their bread going stale in a day. This is undoubtedly true, and no one wants bread to go stale in a day. But notice how seductive the fallacy is: The statement itself is true, but the real reason involves the processing of the grains, which removes all the *natural* ingredients that would preserve it. And anyone who has ever had homemade bread knows that it does not go stale in a day, so blaming our desire for fresh bread is fallacious.

The belief that the use of marijuana leads to the use of heroin is another false cause argument that has been around for a while. Imagine you want to investigate this claim. You go into the field and pay heroin addicts five dollars to answer a questionnaire. One of the questions, "Did you use marijuana before using heroin?" is answered affirmatively by 85 percent of heroin users. Leaving aside questions of honesty, you have found a high correlation between heroin use and previous marijuana use. Put another way, if an individual uses heroin, it is likely he or she previously used marijuana. The big question remains, however: Have you established that marijuana use *leads* to heroin use? Certainly not, since you have not obtained information about marijuana users who did *not* go on to heroin. Today we know that the vast majority of marijuana users never go on to heroin, but 20 years ago this was not so obvious—those who knew were not talking.

You can always get the results you want.
Just ask the right questions
to the right people.

Another way to illustrate the faulty relationship between the two sets of data is to introduce a third. Suppose you asked the question, "Did you smoke cigarettes before using heroin?" Again the correlation turns out to be 85 percent. What have you found now? Just as much as before: If you use heroin it is likely that you previously smoked cigarettes. Changing the example still further, you might question alcoholics about their previous consumption of milk. Of course you would find a tremendously high correlation there. But in this case you know that far more people who drank milk never became alcoholics, so the suggestion is dismissed. But isn't it impressive that every alcoholic used to drink milk? It should not be.

Attack a false cause in two ways:
First, find other causes;
second, find other false correlations.

These are the best two ways to attack false causes: First, by coming up with a different reasonable cause, you show that there may be other explanations. Next, you compare the explanation offered to other simplistic explanations or correlations. A too-simple explanation we all used to believe is that the Civil War was fought to end slavery; only later in life did we learn the other, economic reasons. Similarly, with Columbus's discovery of the New World: The simple, false explanation or cause was that he wanted to prove the world was round. The truth is far more commercial: He was looking for a short, inexpensive trade route to India. These examples do not show that the opposer is wrong, just that causes must be defended.

---

*There is no such thing as
the cause of something.*

This last point is meant to save anyone so foolish as to claim that *one* thing is *THE* cause of another. When cornered, you should simply agree that nothing has a unique, single cause. That does not mean one cause is not crucial: "Of course," you magnanimously agree, "nothing is the cause of vandalism. Nonetheless, the lack of parental supervision is a contributing factor, don't you think?" Since any unfavorable social condition will encourage vandalism, the statement can hardly prompt disagreement.

The last of the three fallacies in this chapter is the fallacy of *hasty generalization*. It is not unusual to hear someone reply to a statement with "That's just a generalization!" But there is no reason to dismiss a statement just because it is a generalization:

> JOSH: Don't believe a word he says—he's running for office, and people running for office make false promises.

ANNE-LISE: That's a generalization.

JOSH: So?

Merely pointing out that a statement is general may be interesting, but it hardly provides a reason for dismissing it. Should someone react to one of your statements in this way, reply as Anne-Lise did and wait for an answer.

The explanation for our prejudice against generalizations is the frequency with which they are made too quickly and on poor evidence. They are often far too broad and sweeping. In addition, they are easy to knock down: Generalizations require only one exception to be proven wrong. The statement, for example, that all teachers are afraid of the real world turns out to be false if you can find one teacher without this fear.

> *One exception*
> *falsifies a generalization.*

There is a saying, "It is the exception that proves the rule," that is sometimes produced in response to a counterexample. Someone says, as did a letter-writer to a news magazine, "Everyone thinks he can get away with anything." Our Hero, who happens to be lurking in a doorway, comes to the rescue:

LAUREN: Everyone thinks they can get away with anything.

OUR HERO: I don't. If I thought that, I would never pay taxes, for one thing.

LAUREN: Well, that's just the exception that proves the rule.

OUR HERO: No it isn't. It's the exception that falsifies the generalization.

LAUREN: Everyone knows there are exceptions to any statement.

OUR HERO: That old saying means just the opposite of what you think. It means that the rule is false if it has exceptions. The original statement is Scottish and meant the opposite of what it sounds like in modern English.

LAUREN: Well, it's still true that every generalization has exceptions.

OUR HERO: How many? How much do you want to qualify that statement?

LAUREN: Most people think they can get away with everything. How's that?

OUR HERO: False. I don't think you're right. Maybe most people think they can get away with *something*—say, not paying a parking ticket or something like that; but by and large most people figure they'll be caught if they do anything wrong.

LAUREN: Well, *some* people think they can get away with anything.

OUR HERO: That's probably right.

Lauren has been driven back to a much weaker statement. The fallacy of hasty generalization occurs when a statement goes beyond the evidence supporting it.

Very few statements are universally true, so always put a rider on a statement rather than be forced to take it back later. Instead of saying "All politicians are crooks," try "An awful lot of politicians are crooks." The latter is a much easier statement to defend.

> *Never make a general statement stronger than you need to— you may be forced to retract.*

We are all familiar with the sorts of qualifiers normally used: "By and large," "just about all . . . ," "most," and so on. These expressions are very vague: "By and large all professors are dull." How many interesting professors are required to make that statement false?

MATT: Professors are dull.

OUR HERO: Do you mean *all* professors?

MATT: No. But most of them are dull.

OUR HERO: How many is *most*? 75 percent? 95 percent?

MATT: Something like that.

OUR HERO: How many professors have you known? Fifty or sixty? Maybe you've been unlucky.

MATT: That's possible, but I don't think so.

OUR HERO: Why?

Matt is required to defend a statement he probably never meant seriously in the first place. Much to Matt's surprise, Our Hero listened to what he said. Our Hero, knowing that most people speak without thinking, will probably win this argument easily. The key to winning, as always, is listening.

22

Three Sneaky Moves

The last three fallacies to be presented are the fallacy of false dilemma, the fallacy of "two wrongs" or common practice, and the fallacy of appeal to force. They are all common maneuvers and should be high on your list of tactics to watch for.

A dilemma is a situation in which you must make a choice between alternatives. Very often there is no difficulty at all in making choices, while at other times the decision can present quite a problem. Usually, saying that someone is facing a dilemma means that she must make a difficult choice. In fact all choices are dilemmas, but we tend to save the name "dilemma" for the hard ones. The question now is, when is a dilemma a **false dilemma**? Put another way, the answer is obvious: When is a decision between two alternatives phony? Answer: when there are really more than two alternatives.

Be suspicious of choices:
Are there really more
than you have been offered?

A **false dilemma** is a maneuver that attempts to limit the number of choices in a given situation. A famous slogan of the Vietnam era, "America—Love It or Leave It," was based on a false dilemma. Why are *loving* and *leaving* the only two choices? Surely there are others. Observe Sophie trying to con Our Hero:

SOPHIE: Excuse me. Would you care to sign this petition?

OUR HERO: What's it about?

SOPHIE: It demands the government make cigarette smoking illegal.

OUR HERO: Well, I don't think I will sign, thank you.

SOPHIE: Oh, so you don't care who gets cancer?

OUR HERO: Are those your only alternatives: either sign or you're in favor of cancer?

SOPHIE: What if they are?

OUR HERO: It's a lousy argument, that's what. There are many people including myself who are not smokers but who would not sign your petition. You are just offering a false dilemma.

Sophie may not be impressed by this attack, but Our Hero is correct: The alternatives have been unfairly limited to two.

It is very common, when false dilemmas are introduced, to have one of the two choices be the obvious favorite. This is usually done by phrasing the two alternatives in highly leading language. There was a heated debate recently in Toronto concerning the musical *Showboat*. Some groups claimed that the show was racist and should not be supported by public funds, and that no one ought to see the show. According to some of them, anyone who did buy a ticket was racist: so, either you boycotted the show or you were a racist. What a choice! There are many alternatives between the two laid out. One might believe the show is not racist, or that it is but is historically important, or that such shows must be seen and understood in context. It can easily be seen why this fallacy is sometimes called the fallacy of **black-and-white**—everything is put into final one-or-the-other terms.

Political parties, whether in power or out, often use the fallacy of false dilemma to frighten people: "Either support us or suffer terrible consequences." The U.S. National Rifle Association keeps claiming that either citizens have easy access to firearms or the United States will be controlled by criminals. One alternative has people running around with everything from derringers to machine guns, and the other has a defenseless population cowering fearfully in their bedrooms. Is there no position between the two? What about stricter controls that do not completely eliminate gun ownership? What about limiting ownership to police forces and increasing penalties for carrying illegal firearms? These are all possibilities that the dilemma tries to ignore.

Another example of false dilemma frequently occurs in debates that pit ecological issues against economic concerns. The so-called green side claims that, unless the environment is completely protected and left untouched, we will all perish like the dinosaurs. On the other side, industrialists and developers point to the children of unemployed workers who will starve or be on welfare unless the forests and the oceans are denuded. The choices you are given are either the destruction of the planet or the ruination of a community. No wonder it's a hard argument.

Remember, in the fight for your opinion, the fallacy of false dilemma is a potent weapon.

> *When the choices seem extreme*
> *look in the middle.*

The next fallacy is that of **two wrongs**, or *common practice*. In this fallacy the justification for bad actions is that others do it. One argument that always seems to bring out this fallacy concerns corporate bribery in foreign countries. Executives argue that when doing business in many countries it is necessary to use bribes because that is what is done there; unless we do it too, they argue, we'll lose business and jobs. This statement incorporates the fallacy of two wrongs. The argument against paying bribes is that bribery is wrong. The executives' counter-argument that these payments are a common practice is irrelevant to the claim that bribery is immoral. The fact that everyone does it is not enough to make it right.

> *Replies appealing to common practice*
> *are almost always irrelevant.*

Another sort of appeal justifies something wrong by pointing to something else that is also wrong. A boss might refuse a reasonable request for a raise by pointing out that several employees were recently laid off: "How would it

133

look if you were given a raise when others were laid off?"
This is the fallacy of two wrongs. It was unfortunate that
others were laid off, but that is not really relevant to your
raise. (It would be relevant if the boss pointed out that there
simply was no money, but that was not the argument.) Some
(but not all) arguments for affirmative action defend discrimination against men on the grounds that there is discrimination against women. There are other, nonfallacious
arguments that depend on the notions of historical redress
and the need to correct current imbalances, but defending
discrimination against men simply because there is discrimination against women is like defending violence against men
because there is violence against women. More violence
doesn't help anyone.

The following dialogue also illustrates the fallacy:

DIDI: The police must be given broader powers to
stop organized crime.

OUR HERO: While I would like to see organized crime
stopped, I'm afraid such powers might be abused.

DIDI: You can't make an omelette without breaking a
few eggs. Some people might be hurt, but that
can't be helped.

OUR HERO: I think that requires some defense, Didi.
What's the point of stopping crime if people will
be hurt? After all, we want to stop crime because
it hurts people.

DIDI: Fewer people will be hurt by the police than by
criminals.

OUR HERO: I think that's true. But if anyone is hurt by
the police, it's wrong. If we remove rights, we have
changed the whole system we are trying to protect
in the first place. Two wrongs do not make a right:

Just because the crooks are doing nasty things does not mean that we should.

This argument is liable to continue for some time. Simply pointing out that a fallacy has been committed may not stop your opposer: A very good reason for abandoning the argument must be presented. Our Hero is correct that the argument is a two wrongs fallacy. Didi may still have a chance to make her case if she thinks quickly, but I would bet on Our Hero. Our Hero might, for example, point out that Didi's solution is like eliminating poverty by shooting all the poor people—it is a solution, but at what cost?

Another form of the two wrongs fallacy argues that, while an action is not good, it is not as bad as some other action. In a letter to the editor, a reader argued that industrialized countries have no right to protest the destruction of the Brazilian rain forests because we also cut down trees here in North America. But even if the scale were the same, the fact that trees are being cut in North America does not mean they should be cut everywhere. That would be like saying that, since many big bank robbers get away with their crimes, lesser criminals should be allowed to hold up corner stores. The commission of one evil does not permit the commission of another.

> *The use of "two wrongs" is an admission of guilt.*

In the following dialogue the above tip is demonstrated by Our Hero:

LAUREN: Certainly violence is justified when its revolutionary aims are valuable.

OUR HERO: But won't innocent people get hurt?

LAUREN: That may happen. But remember, the existing government is also hurting innocent people.

OUR HERO: Is that one reason you oppose them?

LAUREN: Certainly. The revolution will benefit those now being hurt.

OUR HERO: Since, as you've already said, innocent people will be hurt, and that is one reason for your revolution, how can you possibly justify actions that will lead to the same evil? You are saying since they do it, you can do it as well. Yet, at the same time, you claim to be better than they are. That's confusing.

You can have doubts as to Our Hero's revolution-stopping capabilities—not because he argues poorly, but because Lauren does not argue well.

Two wrongs or common practice is often used to justify petty crimes such as taking stationery home from work. Everyone does it, so why shouldn't I? The fact that everyone does it is irrelevant, however; it is the nature of the act, the degree of wrong that accounts for our attitude, not how common it is. In some places, for example, vandalism is quite common, yet people still know it is wrong.

MATTHEW: Don't buy a pen. I can get you one from my office.

OUR HERO: That's stealing.

MATTHEW: No, don't be silly. Everyone takes stuff home from the office.

OUR HERO: I know, but it's stealing.

MATTHEW: It's more like a fringe benefit.

OUR HERO: Oh, then you declare it on your income taxes?

MATTHEW: Of course not. Look. . . .

OUR HERO: Wait. Do you do it openly in front of your boss or co-workers?

MATTHEW: No. That's now how it's done.

OUR HERO: Sounds like stealing to me.

MATTHEW: Everyone does it.

OUR HERO: OK, so we agree that everyone steals. I just don't know if it's such a good idea.

Now Matthew and Our Hero have something to argue about: Is petty theft something that is wrong? That argument might end up either way, and it should be a good one. Notice that Our Hero first tackled the job of getting office theft classed as stealing. This is valuable since calling it by any other name would confuse the issue. Also notice that if Our Hero were to continue the argument, or rather try to end it, with something like, "Well then, since stealing is wrong, what you're doing is wrong," Matthew would be wise to jump on him for begging the question. Having the activity classed as stealing does not automatically mean that it is wrong. (Imagine someone stealing a murderer's gun: that would certainly *not* be wrong.)

The third fallacy dealt with in this chapter, is **appeal to force**, known in Latin circles as the *argumentum ad baculum*. Any threat to loss of life, health, wealth, freedom, and so on is an appeal to force. The basis of an appeal to force is fear. It might be to fear of the unknown, as in religious appeals; it might be to fear of foreigners, as in patriotic appeals; or it might be to fear of harm or danger, as in many perfectly reasonable appeals.

Not every appeal to force is improper. If, for example, you are about to embark on a voyage in a leaky ship and someone says you ought not go because you will drown, you have an appeal to force through the fear of death. However, in general, when a mugger says, "Your money or your life," there is an appeal to force that most of us would respect. The mugger does not deserve the money, but you should give it to him nonetheless.

A threat is never a good reason to believe something, but it may be a good reason to do something.

An employee, arguing with her boss over the company donation to the annual picnic, is correct in watching for the darkening of visage and drawing of brows indicating the boss's loss of temper. As the issue gathers importance she may want to push things further, but always remember that she is usually better off returning to the fray with new arguments, new data, and her job still secure.

An appeal to force is fallacious because it ignores what is right and wrong, true or false. Using threats comes down to saying "No more arguments, no more investigations, the case is closed!" But the case is never closed because nothing is ever certain. The expression "power politics" has a very nice ring to it, but it refers to arguments from force. According to author Philip Deane, when Lyndon Johnson was President he once used this argument to convince the Greek ambassador to favor a U.S. proposal about Cyprus. Deane quoted Johnson as follows: "[*Obscenity*] your Parliament and Constitution. America is an elephant. Cyprus is a flea. Greece is a flea. If those two fleas continue itching the elephant, they might just get whacked by the elephant's trunk, whacked good."* Even if the ambassador did not like the U.S. proposal, this threat may have persuaded him to accept Johnson's point of view. Johnson's argument was fallacious because the threat had nothing to do with the proposal.

Personal relationships, like diplomatic relations between countries, sometimes involve threats of varying kinds. The greatest difficulty with using force in an argument is that it achieves only a temporary victory. As soon as the threat of force is removed, the opponent will go back to his original position, often with renewed fervor. Even countries that use the threat of force find themselves with fierce partners and precarious victories that constantly require attention and vigilance. When this is done in personal argumentation, the results can be not only disastrous, but tiring and isolating as well.

> *Force may end an argument—*
> *but the result will not endure.*

Fears are very easy things to prey on—we all feel insecure about our intellectual, social, and sexual prowess. By feeding on these more or less hidden fears, advertising is able to persuade us through totally irrelevant reasons. We

---

*Toronto Globe and Mail, June 5, 1976.

purchase cars that are expensive and flashy, cosmetics that will make us sexy and attractive, and furnishings that will enhance our prestige. Ads for Scotch whiskey point out that people will notice what brand you serve: You dare not serve the inferior brand lest people suppose you cannot afford better.

When looking at an advertisement
always ask yourself,
what is the ad really selling?

In most cases what is being touted in the ad is irrelevant to the actual product. An ad for Old Grand-Dad Whiskey stated in huge letters, "If not for yourself, for your image." The ad may just as well have stated, "No matter what the stuff tastes like you should still use it!" Another ad, for Bushmills Irish Whiskey, simply pointed out that, "You can tell a lot about an individual by what he pours into his glass." (You can also tell a lot by *how much* he pours in his glass, but the ad says nothing about that.) Cosmetics ads with sexual suggestions also give irrelevant reasons: There is no claim that the product will do anything, but the whole ad conveys a sexual feeling. Age is one of the strongest advertising cudgels around these days. No one wants to get old, and the advertisers know this and prey on our fear of aging. These techniques illustrate that we must be very careful in reading advertisements. Whether you like it or not, you *are* affected by these ads. Since their appeal is largely unconscious, you cannot help it.

When a threat is made, explicitly or implicitly, think before being frightened.

*Is the threat
something to be feared?*

Once, many of us were afraid of ghosts; after all, they are scary. Many of our fears are just as poorly founded, so think before accepting this fallacy.

23

Part Two Review

QUESTIONS

Ask yourself these questions to see how much information you've absorbed.

What fallacy, if any, do you see in the following examples, and what should the next step be?

1. "So now," Arnie said, "the schools are encouraging young kids to have sex."

   "What? They are?" Carole replied.

   "Sure they're supplying them with condoms and instructions on how to use them. Next thing they'll be giving them beds."

2. "Violence on television is rampant," Larry said. "It's permeating our society and teaching our kids all the wrong things."

"So you're suggesting, like, censorship or something?" Peggy asked.

"It's got to be stopped. I mean, don't you think there's too much violence in our society?"

"Well, there sure is. It's getting worse and worse all the time."

"You see, that's exactly my point."

3. ROBERT: Of course the Mayor wants the new subway built along Goatherd Avenue—he and all his friends own a lot of property there.

STEVE: I didn't know that.

ROBERT: Well, you may be the only person left who doesn't. I mean, there's no other reason to pick that street, right?

4. PETER: So, Ms. Rose, am I getting the promotion or not?

MS. ROSE: No, I'm afraid, Peter, that you were not our first choice for the promotion.

PETER: But why not? I thought I was a strong candidate.

MS. ROSE: We just felt you weren't right for the job.

5. "Look at the lineup for that restaurant," Sharon said. "Let's try it next Saturday for our anniversary."

6. "I knew it," Shirley cried, her eyes brimming with tears. "You don't love me! You never did!"

"What are you talking about?" Alex asked, thoroughly perplexed. "Of course I love you. Aren't I taking you to the prom?"

"If you loved me you never would have forgotten."

"Forgotten? Forgotten what?"

Shirley wells over with emotion and a huge sob escapes: "Today's our three month anniversary, and you didn't remember!"

7. "Good gosh," Sean exclaimed. "Did you see what those people were eating?"

"Yes. It looked like muck with chicken beaks in it," Sheila agreed.

"It just goes to show what kind of people they are."

"Too true. Now let's hurry home for lunch. I think there's some leftover haggis in the fridge."

8. "I never said that!"

"Oh, yes you did!"

"I did not. I would never say anything like that."

"You said it. In fact you said it twice. And the second time you were shouting!"

"It's not true. I never said it. And you're the one who's shouting."

"I am not shouting. You are. You're always shouting."

"I never shout. You're the one who always shouts first."

"That's a lie. . . .

9. John Drache has a computer problem. He can't figure out how to get his new printer to work. He complains to Joan, a co-worker, and she advises him to check his word processor to see if the correct printer is listed. John unhesitatingly takes her advice.

10. "I don't know how you can take that astrology garbage seriously. Here, look at this! One of the

world's greatest astronomers, a Nobel Prize winner, was interviewed and called astrology a load
of hooey."

ANSWERS

1. The fallacy of *straw man* occurs when a position
   is exaggerated beyond what its proponents hold.
   Anyone who wants condoms supplied in schools
   would explain that they are just being realistic,
   not promoting sex.

2. But, of course, it wasn't his point. What's happened here is the fallacy of *change of subject* or
   non sequitur, a quick change of subject. Larry,
   perhaps unintentionally, got off the tricky matter
   of censorship and onto the safer ground of anti-
   violence.

3. If you picked *attacking the person* or *argumentum ad hominem*, then you were right. Robert's
   first claim, that the mayor owns property along
   the proposed route, must be shown to be relevant. Further, if you picked *argumentum ad
   populum*, then you are also correct. Robert bol-
   stered his initial claim by stating that "everyone
   knows" about the scam. That might be just another way for Robert to say that *he* believes it. Finally, if you selected the fallacy of *false dilemma*,
   you found the last fallacy. There are undoubtedly
   other reasons in favor of the new subway route,
   but Robert is not interested in hearing them.
   Moral: [a] There can be more than one fallacy in
   even a brief argument; and [b] watch out for
   Robert if you run into him.

4. Peter asked a straightforward question and received a straightforward answer. But when Peter

followed up with a request for reasons, he did not get one. Saying that he's not "right for the job" is just another way of saying he didn't get it. This is the fallacy of *circular reasoning* or *begging the question*, and Peter's best response is to ask why he's not "right" for the job.

5. Sharon, as it turned out, was wrong: The food wasn't good at all. The crowds came to see the ex-football player who owned the place. Her mistake was to fall for the *popularity* fallacy, *argumentum ad populum*—the fallacy that because something is popular it is good or true.

6. While Shirley may or may not be justified in her disappointment with Alex's forgetfulness, her assumption about his lack of love for her is a *hasty conclusion*.

7. When you think you are somehow better than others, you commit the fallacy of *provincialism*. Every culture produces food (such as this unusual Scottish dish) treated as delicacies by insiders and appalling by outsiders.

8. In arguments like this one, sadly familiar to many of us, one of the biggest problems is the constant *changing of subject—non sequiturs* flow like water. Let's hope that things will eventually simmer down and the real issues will be broached.

9. One might suspect an *ad verecundiam, appeal to authority* has been committed, but it has not. On everyday matters it is perfectly appropriate to take the advice of someone who knows more than you do—even if your only evidence is that they sound like they know what they're talking about. Joan might, after all, save John a trip to the computer store.

10. First of all, the statement is *not* a fallacious *appeal to authority*. An expert in astronomy is entitled to have an opinion on astrology, which is worth attending to. What this statement might be is a *circular argument*, but what it really is is a good reason to question astrology. By the way, what's your sign?

The Arguments

24

Pot Luck

PAUL: Lord, I wish they'd legalize marijuana.

CHLOE: Are you sure that's a good idea?

> Good. Chloe thus responds to Paul's claim with a question, not with another statement. This is the right way.

PAUL: Sure I'm sure. Don't tell me you think it should be illegal! You must be the last person in the world to believe that.

> Paul is trying to intimidate Chloe: Being the last person to agree means being "out of it." This is a fallacy. Notice that Paul has not yet given a reason for his position.

CHLOE: If I'm the last person, how come it's still illegal? I'd like to know why it should be legal. After all, there's no proof it isn't harmful.

> Good. This is an excellent response to the fallacy.

> Mistake. Chloe has offered a reason when she did not have to—she did not start the argument. If Paul attacks, Chloe may be on the defensive.

PAUL: How much proof is needed? Marijuana must be the most tested drug in history. They've been trying to find something wrong with it for years. Why should marijuana need more testing than anything else?

CHLOE: Because it is taken for pleasure, not out of necessity. Other drugs are needed for health, not highs.

> Chloe is solidly on the defensive. She should be ending his answers with questions in order to put Paul on the defensive.

PAUL: So what? Why does the *purpose* matter? Are you saying no drugs should be used for pleasure?

CHLOE: They should be used as little as possible altogether. It just isn't a good idea to put foreign substances into our bodies. When it comes to medicine, it may be necessary. But why risk health for pleasure?

> Paul has identified Chloe's principle (drugs for pleasure are bad), and Chloe has agreed.

PAUL: What about alcohol? That's a drug used for pleasure, and it's legal.

> Paul is appealing to the Principle of Similar Cases.

CHLOE: I personally don't think it should be legal. I would make booze illegal rather than make grass legal.

> Good. Any other answer would have led to trouble. Trying to distinguish between alcohol and marijuana would be hard.

PAUL: But you drink!

> Oops! Paul made a statement and did not ask a question. Chloe may be able to grab the offensive.

CHLOE: So what?

PAUL: I suppose that's not important. Don't you think the choice to protect our bodies from all these chemicals should be a personal decision? I would rather live a few years less and smoke grass and drink wine. Why shouldn't that be my choice?

> Bravo! Paul realizes he has made a mistake. More important, he realizes it does not matter that Chloe drinks. Rather than try to defend his point, he quickly gives it up and moves on to more fruitful fields. Chloe should have made her attack stronger.

CHLOE: Because one function of society is to protect its members.

PAUL: To what degree? I'm delighted that poison can't be sold as vitamins and that milk must be clean. But surely we must be allowed some choices. Why not make candy illegal?

Chloe has introduced a new principle (that society must protect its members), so Paul needs a new counter-example. He wants to show that Chloe does not really accept that principle.

CHLOE: Don't be silly.

A reply like this means that Chloe cannot think of an answer. It is a signal for Paul to move in.

PAUL: I'm not being silly. Candy is bad for us. It rots our teeth, makes us fat, keeps us from eating properly, and contains dozens of artificial things. Not only that, but the main users are children. Think of it, Chloe, *children*! Why shouldn't we make it illegal?

CHLOE: Candy is different. I agree that chemicals in it should be taken out, but it's in a different class.

Chloe has still not pointed to a difference between candy and marijuana.

PAUL: But you still haven't told me how candy is different. Why should one thing that's bad be legal and another illegal?

Good. Paul has noticed that Chloe did not answer the question.

CHLOE: I don't know. I just hate the idea of legalizing another way of damaging our bodies. Why should we increase the number of bad things?

Chloe has lost. She cannot make the distinction. There may be one, but Chloe cannot find it and knows she is in trouble. Since she has no defense, she tries to take the offense by asking a question. She is also accusing Paul of committing the fallacy of "two wrongs make a right."

PAUL: I don't think we are increasing the number of bad things. I don't think grass is bad. You want to penalize one segment of society because the stuff they like came along later than booze and candy. That's just not fair.

Paul rejects Chloe's charge by denying grass is bad. He remembers that marijuana's being unhealthy was an *assumption* he granted Chloe for the sake of argument. Chloe borrowed the fact that marijuana is bad; she never proved that it was bad.

25

The Gay Life

JACOB: Did you read about that guy who was drummed out of the army for being an open homosexual?

DANIEL: Yeah. I'd like to see more of that. This whole business of it being all right is nuts. Did you think he should *not* have been kicked out?

JACOB: Gee, it's not nearly so clear to me. What makes you so sure the army is right?

Good. All too often we defend a position we are not really sure of. This always tends to lead to trouble. We are much better off saying we are not sure and letting the opposer carry the ball.

DANIEL: Well, I just think it's getting to the point where we have to do something or our kids will end up thinking it's normal to be queer. You don't want your kids to be queer, do you?

JACOB: Well, I guess I rather they weren't gay. What bothers me is the connection. You seem so sure about these kids becoming gay. Why?

Daniel's intimidating question incorporated an appeal to fear. Jacob handles it well here by not giving it a big play.

DANIEL: Don't be naive, Jacob. Even the President backed down on it. Would he risk changing his mind if he weren't convinced?

This is the fallacy of appealing to authority. The U.S. President is not an expert on homosexuality, only on popular opinion.

JACOB: Maybe, and maybe not. But I need persuading. I can't see taking away someone's rights without a damn good reason. The next thing you know they'll go after bachelors!

Jacob is not getting anywhere. His next move is to bring his point home by applying it to a case Daniel will care about. He also handled the fallacy of authority very nicely.

DANIEL: Come off it! What are you talking about?

JACOB: Look, the army says it can fire this guy because he's queer. Well, that means they're firing him because of what he does with some other people on his own time. So what's to stop them from firing me for sleeping with women?

Now Jacob has made his point clearly, so it is a good time for a question. Daniel will have to deal with Jacob's argument sooner or later. ·

DANIEL: Why would they do that?

Daniel could not think of a quick answer, so he replied with a question. This is about the best move there is when a quick response is needed.

JACOB: Maybe because there's a lot more women in the army now. It doesn't really matter. If they can throw this guy out, what about me? And you don't stay home alone every night yourself, my boy!

DANIEL: There are laws to stop that sort of thing. It doesn't make sense to fire someone for sleeping with a girlfriend—everyone does it.

There are two separate fallacies in this response. The first is begging the question: Why shouldn't the laws protecting heterosexual couples also protect homosexual couples? The second fallacy is the *two wrongs* or *common practice* fallacy: The fact that everyone sleeps with his girlfriend does not make it right.

JACOB: Well, then, why aren't there laws to stop homosexuals from being fired? A lot of people are gay.

DANIEL: That's different. It's not normal.

JACOB: Maybe it isn't the norm, but is it wrong? Are guys getting fired for no good reason?

Jacob does not want to argue about the meaning of "normal" and neatly avoids the issue. His use of the hedge expression "maybe" means that he can retract the statement later if he needs to.

DANIEL: Look, Jake, the more acceptance of gays there is, the more chance there is the kids will get turned on to it. That's the thing that really worries me!

JACOB: But the psychologists say that a kid's sexual orientation is set by the time he's five. That's before a lot of contact out of the home. How about that?

DANIEL: That's fine for psychologists! Maybe they don't have kids.

This statement is completely irrelevant—having kids has nothing to do with expertise.

Anyway, the shrinks are the ones always letting killers out of jail, aren't they?

This is slightly better since it reflects on the reliability of psychologists.

JACOB: We're getting nowhere fast, Daniel. We don't even know if the guy in the military had anything to do with kids. If he didn't, do you still think he should be fired?

Notice that Jacob is not conceding the point with his question. All he is doing is trying to clarify and narrow Daniel's claim. The issue will now depend on Daniel's answer.

157

DANIEL: Well, I suppose in the army he wouldn't have a lot of contact with kids, so maybe he shouldn't be fired. But gays shouldn't be allowed near kids.

JACOB: Why not? What are they going to do? Do you think all gays are child molesters?

Now that one route has been selected, it can be examined more closely.

DANIEL: Probably not, but it wouldn't shock me. What I'm afraid of is the kids imitating them. Teachers, for instance, have a great effect on kids. If that would make a difference, then I say fire them.

JACOB: Well, I don't know enough about that. We need some experts there, I guess. But still, by whose lights would the effect be bad?

Neither disputant is able to argue the technical points, so they will move on to the more general issue.

DANIEL: *My* lights. Frankly, Jacob, the whole idea of homosexuality scares the hell out of me. I don't care if my attitude is wrong, I want it done and I'm not willing to argue about it.

It is a good technique to announce when argument will no longer help. It is fair to your opposer and keeps the argument from getting too heated.

JACOB: All right, my friend, I won't push the point. I'm just worried that you're being paranoid and unfair.

Jacob is respecting Daniel's desire to stop. He leaves Daniel with a thought that neatly captures his main point.

26

Equal Rights for Equal Arguments

KRISTA: I decided to apply for the policewoman's job.

MARK: What? I think you're nuts.

KRISTA: Nuts? Why am I nuts?

> Good. Instead of reacting, Krista treats the "nuts" statement as a claim.

MARK: Women don't belong on the police force. I mean, they can't go running after robbers and muggers, can they?

KRISTA: Why not?

> Still the right move. The immediate temptation to go on the attack is very strong, but should be resisted. By asking a question, Krista gets a better idea of what to attack.

MARK: [*Chuckling*] Heh, heh. Who'd save the cops from the bad guys?

Mark has not said anything new; he is just repeating what he said already. His comments should not be treated as a reason, but as a conclusion. Krista's response is correct.

KRISTA: What makes you think that would happen?

MARK: Come on, Krista. Most men could make mincemeat of most women. How can women be expected to subdue criminals and arrest them?

KRISTA: You think men would have an easier time arresting criminals than women would? Is that right?

Krista wants the argument to be precise. The best way to do this is to get the agreement of your argument partner on the issue.

MARK: Exactly, I just can't see how. . . .

KRISTA: Wait. I want to get straight on this. If I can convince you that a woman can have as easy a time as a man in an arrest situation, then you'll agree?

A good interruption. Mark was likely just going to repeat himself again. A very powerful move, and one that attempts to make the rules of the game perfectly clear.

MARK: Sure. You convince me that any woman will have as easy a time and you're in.

KRISTA: No. Not *any* woman. Any woman who wants to be a cop and meets the requirements. After all, there are lots of guys who would have trouble arresting a kid.

Mark, intentionally or not, distorted Krista's position. Krista noticed the *straw-man* fallacy and reacted.

MARK: OK, you're on.
[*Krista reaches over to Mark, grabs his arm and flips him over. He ends up on the floor, and Krista has a firm hammerlock on him. Since this conversation is taking place in New York, no one else in the bar has noticed.*]

This is known as nonverbal communication. Krista has demonstrated a fact, but which fact is still open to debate.

MARK: What the hell! You're crazy! Get off me!

KRISTA: Well, do you agree a woman can arrest a man?

MARK: No, I don't! Just because you threw me doesn't mean I have to agree. You took me by surprise. I agree you threw me, but that doesn't mean a woman can throw a man whenever she wants. I wasn't ready.

Good. Mark recovered his wits, and he is not letting Krista make a *hasty generalization*.

KRISTA: Are you ready now?

MARK: No! Don't! I admit you can throw me whenever you want to, but that's still doesn't make the point.

KRISTA: Oh, but Mark, it does. Don't you see? Why can I throw you? I'm not bigger than you.

Emotion is not out of place in an argument so long as the issues are kept in sight. Showing concern, excitement, or anger is fine if it does not interfere with the discussion.

MARK: Because you're a bloody black belt in karate, that's why. Besides, you're mad. What would you do if you ran up against a crook who also studied karate?

This is a sign of retreat. By his question Mark shows he agrees that women could win if trained.

KRISTA: The same thing a male cop would do—call for help! The point is we can be on the same footing.

MARK: Women cops, you know, would lead to more violence. There's no question about it.

A dramatic *change of subject*.

161

KRISTA: What? Why?

Oh, no. Krista did not react to the switch. She may be interested in what Mark said, but she should have tied up the original argument first.

MARK: Well, men have always been the enforcement figures. It is easier for us to obey men since most of us were obedient to fathers. The cop on the beat has a whole historical tradition and psychology to back him up. That's why he survives as well as he does. Women don't have that tradition, so they are more likely to get attacked. When that happens they'll have to use force and guns more often themselves. See what I mean?

A clever move by Mark. His argument is long enough to make his earlier retreat just a memory, and it is complex enough so Krista will have to concentrate on what he is saying.

KRISTA: What sort of drugstore psychology is that? As soon as it is understood that women are not going to take crap when they're cops, they'll have all the respect they need.

This is the fallacy of *attacking the person*. It is not serious, though, because it is followed by reasons.

MARK: But how many people will be hurt while they earn that respect? Anyway, it sounds more like fear to me.

Mark is sticking to his point: Other people will suffer if women are allowed to be cops on the beat.

KRISTA: Mark, that's just the point. Maybe it's necessary to hurt some people in order to get the idea across that women can do anything. It shouldn't be necessary to earn respect, but it is. Does that mean we have to stay home and cook? It's not our fault women aren't respected. Why should we suffer for it?

A good reply to the core of Mark's point. Krista ends with a question Mark cannot answer.

MARK: Well, I just hope you never have to arrest me, that's all.

Mark is admitting defeat. Krista must not demand more of a victory. To insist that her opposer stand up and surrender would be a mistake. Any resentment created by such a demand is liable to interfere with persuasion. The creative approach to argument emphasizes bringing a respondent around to your point of view, not gloating over victories. Always keep in mind the point of arguing: persuasion.

A general point: When Mark changed the subject to women cops leading to more violence, Krista missed the switch. Had she not subsequently won that part of the argument, her first victory might have been forgotten. Always wrap up one part of an argument before changing topics.

27

Why Get Married?

ZACHARY: Why get married? I don't see the point.

JENNIFER: I told you why. It's a way of expressing commitment.

ZACK: I have no qualms about expressing commitment. I've told you over and over that we will be together forever. But why get married?

Zack has accepted the idea that commitment is important. Now the argument should be about the form of the commitment.

JEN: I know you've said it. But I guess that isn't enough.

ZACK: We've been living together for two years. Doesn't that count as a sign?

JEN: Sure, but I still want to get married.

ZACK: What difference would it make?
Nothing would change. Marriage is
just a piece of paper.

JEN: If that's true, why not get married?

Good. After all, Zack is saying it is
no big deal, so. . . .

ZACK: Because I don't like going along
with the system, that's why.

This could be trouble for Zachary.
Notice how the offense has switched
to Jennifer. She is now asking the
questions, while he is providing the
answers. If he runs out of answers, he
may find himself married.

JEN: Nonsense! You work in a law
firm, you belong to clubs, you vote,
you go along with the system right
down the line.

This is a direct rebuttal that makes
use of counter-examples. Zachary must
now provide a different reason, or
show why the examples are not like
marriage.

ZACK: Those are different. I *have* to
work, and if I don't vote, then I'm
not getting a say in society. If we get
married we'll end up like everybody
else. I wish I knew what was going
on with you.

JEN: There's nothing secret going on
with me. I'm spending a lot of years
with you, and I want to know that
we really are planning to do this
forever. The best way I know of
saying that is, "I do."

Jennifer is wise to put her case on
the level of feelings. Trying rational
argument would not work.

ZACK: You always get so extreme
about things.

This is a desperate attempt to
change the subject.

JEN: Did you hear what I just said?

ZACK: Of course.

JEN: What did I say? Tell me.

This is a good way of forcing the
argument back onto the issue.

ZACK: You said you're worried about the future. Right?

JEN: Right. I want to know that you are as committed as I am. You haven't given me one reason for *not* getting married.

ZACK: That's not true. I've given lots.

JEN: Why don't you tell me what's really going on? What are you really feeling?

The fact that the argument is going nowhere is a good sign that feelings and emotions may be involved. Jennifer is correct to stop going in circles and to try to get to the real issues.

ZACK: If you really want to know, the idea of getting married scares the hell out of me. It just frightens me to death.

At this point there should be a discussion between Jen and Zack about their feelings toward marriage. The rational façade was eliminated through argument. No one really had good reasons one way or the other. What they have to do is begin talking about what they feel.

28

Good-Bye, Friends

JASON: Hi, Matt. I just came by to say so long.

MATT: Where are you going? I had no idea you were leaving.

JASON: I'm joining the Starpeople. I move in with them tomorrow.

MATT: What! You're leaving your house? What about your job?

JASON: No. I'm keeping my job, but I'm selling my house and giving the money to the Stars. They need it more than I do. I'm also afraid we won't be able to have lunch together again.

MATT: You're mad! This is crazy! They're taking you for a ride! Have you thought about this?

JASON: We Starpeople believe thinking is wrong. Feeling is all that matters. I feel this is right for me.

This outrageously *begs the question*. By what process does Jason know thinking is wrong, and only feelings matter?

MATT: Jason, I like *feeling* too. I think feeling is great. But how can you trust your feelings all the time? What if they're wrong?

Good. Matt stresses agreement.

JASON: Feelings just are. There's no question of right or wrong.

MATT: Sometimes I feel like I should kill my wife. I get incredibly angry and full of homicidal feelings. That doesn't mean I should do it or even harm her.

Matt is testing Jason's principle. Jason's answer will indicate if it is "Follow all feeling."

JASON: You just have those feelings because you are impure. You don't understand that the only real feeling is love.

This does get Jason out of trouble—but is love the only feeling?

MATT: Love is the *only* feeling? That's the only thing you ever feel?

JASON: Right, Matt. It's beautiful and peaceful.

MATT: What about hate, fear, jealousy, desire, annoyance, exasperation? Don't you ever feel any of those?

JASON: No.

MATT: Sounds boring. You really don't feel anger anymore? If I socked you one, you'd just grin at me? How do you protect yourself?

Matt is going wrong. He should not try to argue about Jason's newfound insights. This won't get anywhere.

168

JASON: There is no need to.

MATT: What about fear? Without fear you might walk off a cliff or something.

JASON: You don't need fear to avoid that—just sense. No. Love is all that's needed.

MATT: Let's leave love alone for a minute. You said you're selling your house and giving them the money, right?

If one avenue of attack is not working, try another.

JASON: Right. I give up my house and two-thirds of my salary.

MATT: I should've guessed. Why do they need all that money?

JASON: It's mostly used for missions to gain converts. Starpeople want the whole world bathed in love. But the other thing is liberating ourselves from material possessions. By giving up my worldly attachments, I can get closer to reality and see its love.

Good. Jason gives two answers—if one does not work, the other may.

MATT: If there are many people in your income bracket involved, we're talking about a hefty sum of money. Who gets all this loot? Someone must be making a good living out of this.

JASON: You really don't understand, Matt. You see everything in commercial terms.

Jason dismisses this comment by attacking Matt's outlook, so the fallacy of *attack to the person* or *argumentum ad hominem* is committed.

MATT: You're not being very open-minded, Jason. If I disagree you say I don't understand. That's not a great attitude for someone whose only feeling is love. I just want to know what's going on.

JASON: I'm sorry, Matt, but you can't really know. You have to feel it, not understand it.

This is a form of the fallacy of *circular reasoning* called *special pleading*. Jason is appealing to special knowledge or insights, and anyone who does not have this special characteristic cannot understand.

MATT: Look, Jason, I feel very bad about this. I'm really all torn up and I want you to try and help me. OK?

Matt is going to try another tack. He sees his line and wants to be sure that Jason will be listening.

JASON: If it's help you want, I'll give it.

MATT: You know I feel you're being ripped off and hoodwinked. Can you understand how I feel?

JASON: Sure. It's difficult with something so strange.

MATT: OK, here's my pitch. Is it possible you are wrong? I mean is it remotely, distantly, somehow possible that you're being conned?

Matt must reiterate this question until he gets a "yes."

JASON: No, Matt, it isn't.

MATT: You don't understand, Jason. I mean is it *possible*; I'm not saying you're wrong. I just want to know if it's possible that somewhere a mistake was made? I mean, nothing is certain in life, is it? You might be wrong? You don't think you are, but you might be?

Matt can keep asking this until Jason is exhausted.

JASON: I suppose it's possible. But it isn't true—I'm not being taken by anyone for anything.

MATT: How would you know if you were? What would change your mind?

Matt must get Jason to specify what evidence Matt needs in order to prove to Jason that the Starpeople are phony.

JASON: I don't know. What are you getting at?

MATT: What if I prove that some of the higher-ups in this organization are making a lot of money for themselves? If I could show that, would you reconsider?

Unfortunately, Matt has had to suggest this evidence. The maneuver may still work, however.

JASON: Well, I don't know.

MATT: You keep saying that, Jason. How about it, are you willing to take a chance? Remember, you think you're right, so you've got nothing to lose. All I want is a promise you'll listen. Have I got it?

JASON: Sure. I don't think you'll find any proof. I'm not afraid to have you look.

MATT: All right, then. I'll meet you here in a week.

Now the rules are set. Through careful argument Matt has a chance to persuade his friend.

29

To See or Not to See

JULIE: Did you see where they convicted the guy who owned the sex shops?

DIANA: No. What was it about?

JULIE: Well, he was selling all sorts of sex aids and stuff. You know, vibrators and whatnot, and the cops came and arrested him for selling and displaying obscene material.

DIANA: You're kidding! And was he convicted?

JULIE: Yes. You sound like you don't approve.

DIANA: I think it's incredible that someone should be convicted of that in our day and age. What has he done wrong?

Good. Julie is now forced to answer the first real question.

JULIE: Well, at the least he sold obscene stuff—that's illegal so he should be arrested.

> This is the fallacy of *begging the question*. If he has done nothing wrong, he should not be arrested.

DIANA: Why should selling the stuff be illegal?

> The correct response. The reason Julie gave (that it is illegal, so he should be arrested) is treated like a conclusion.

JULIE: It's offensive to many people.

DIANA: So what? Should everything that offends people be illegal? Lots of people are still offended by two-piece bathing suits.

> Diana has neatly picked out Julie's principle—things offensive to many people should be illegal. Diana immediately thinks of an example that will not please Julie.

JULIE: That's different. It's just a question of style.

> Julie is now bound, by the Principle of Similar Cases, to show a relevant difference between bathing suits and vibrators.

DIANA: Style? That just means popularity. Why do things have to be accepted? There was a time, you know, when women were arrested for wearing bikinis.

JULIE: But *now* they're not. As tastes change we become more liberal. That's fine.

DIANA: I don't understand what you're getting at.

> Excellent. Diana is confused, and instead of pretending to understand, she tells Julie.

JULIE: I don't think everything should be allowed. The tough part is how to figure where to stop. OK, so we allow bikinis. But should we allow stores to sell vibrators? What about whips and chains? The only way to get it all straightened out is to have fuzzy laws; then, when someone is arrested, we can let the courts try it.

DIANA: That just comes down to letting the minority set standards for the majority.

This is not at all what Julie said. It is the fallacy of the *straw man*, a distortion.

JULIE: So? What's wrong with that?

Julie has missed the fallacy, but she has been quick enough to question Diana's claim. All too often we never question the obvious.

DIANA: I don't know. I guess I never thought about it.

JULIE: Standards have to be set. The way we set up our government is letting one group lead us. That's democracy.

DIANA: No, there's a difference. Wait a minute, let me think. . . . [*After a minute.*] Look, the people who convicted the guy were not elected, they were just chosen as a jury, right?

A valuable move. Taking a minute to think can make an amazing difference. No one ever said an argument cannot be stopped for a think-break.

JULIE: Right. So what?

DIANA: Well, now. Suppose you and I and a couple of our friends had been on the jury. None of us is bothered by the stuff that guy was selling. You may approve of censorship, but you don't really care about vibrators. Correct?

Diana carefully gets Julie's agreement at each step. This will prevent Julie from complaining later.

JULIE: That's right. Personally that equipment doesn't bother me.

DIANA: So, if we were on the jury, he wouldn't have been convicted. We would at least have kept him from a guilty verdict, right?

JULIE: I suppose so, but what are you getting at?

DIANA: Just this. His conviction has nothing to do with right and wrong, good and bad. He was unlucky to have a conservative jury. There is no justice here, just luck. I think that stinks.

JULIE: When you put it that way, I have to agree. But I still feel there should be some limits. And anyway, isn't the whole jury system a question of luck?

Julie knows she is caught. But she remembers her position and wisely returns to it.

DIANA: I guess so, to a certain extent. But in this case the jury had to decide if there was a crime at all. I think that's what happens when we try to legislates taste.

175

30

The Mark Market

ROBBIE: Hey, Claire, where you hurrying off to?

CLAIRE: [*Looks around to make sure she's not overheard.*] Well, actually, I've got to get over to the essay service to pick up something they did for me.

ROBBIE: [*Loudly.*] You're going to an essay service!?!

CLAIRE: Quiet! Yeah, I am. So what?

ROBBIE: Well, it's wrong, that's what.

Robbie would have done better had he first asked Claire why she was doing it.

CLAIRE: What's so wrong about it?

See? Now Robbie is defending.

ROBBIE: It's cheating, Claire. That's wrong.

This actually *begs the question* since it's really another way of saying that using an essay service is wrong.

CLAIRE: It's not cheating. It's creative time management.

> Claire should have kept Robbie on the defensive, but she hasn't.

ROBBIE: That's BS. And if it's not cheating, how come you whispered when you talked about it?

> Good. Now Robbie's questioning. He's also pointing up an important discrepancy between words and behavior.

CLAIRE: C'mon! Everybody does it, you know that.

> The fallacy of ad populum, committed here, is often used in this situation.

ROBBIE: I don't do it, and all I know is that it's cheating.

> Good. Robbie used himself as the counter-example.

CLAIRE: [*Sounding stressed.*] You're just being a rule-monger. You don't follow every little rule.

> This is a *change of subject*, from what Claire is doing to what Robbie does or doesn't do.

ROBBIE: That's not the point. This rule is for you. The reason you're in school is to learn; if someone writes your essays for you, then you're not learning anything.

> Good. Robbie didn't bite.

> Robbie has now presented a position that, given how things are going, may not be a bad idea.

CLAIRE: I'm learning plenty. Just because I don't *do* everything doesn't mean I'm not learning.

ROBBIE: You sure didn't learn anything about this assignment. And, besides being unfair to you, it's not fair to everyone else.

CLAIRE: What's it got to do with anyone else?

> Good. If you don't understand, ask.

ROBBIE: Well, look, I don't have as much money as you have, so I have to write my stuff, meet deadlines, and so on. Just because you're rich, you don't have to. That's not fair.

CLAIRE: I also get to drive to school because I can afford a car. Is that unfair?

> A good response. Notice how the example addresses the Principle Principle and uses the Principle of Similar Cases.

ROBBIE: You know that's not the same; driving isn't cheating. What about the class curve? If you've got some unemployed Ph.D. writing an undergrad essay for you, everyone else is going to look bad. You'll get an 'A' and we'll look like simpletons.

> Robbie shows the difference between the two, and then quickly moves on.
>
> This argument refers to Robbie's own interest in the matter, and this makes it stronger.

CLAIRE: Well, I don't know. [*More stress is starting to show.*] Why are you making a federal case out of it?

> Claire does not have a good answer and would like to beg off the argument.

ROBBIE: Because cheating affects us all. You think it's only got to do with you but. . . .

> Robbie is staying with what worked.

CLAIRE: All right, all right! So I'm cheating a little. What's the big deal? I was so stressed out. . . . [*Tears show in Claire's eyes.*]

> OK, so Robbie has an admission, but that's not the most important information that was passed.

ROBBIE: Hey, yeah, don't worry, I'm not going to report you. But what do you mean about the stress?

> Good. Robbie's paying attention to what might really be going on.

CLAIRE: Oh, it was just everything at once. My mother. . . .

> The argument has moved from Claire's tactical defense to a deeper level. Now Robbie might be able to understand both why Claire did what she did and get a commitment that she won't do it again. Claire might benefit from sharing with Robbie, and even get some help in dealing with her stress.

31

To Therapy or Not to Therapy

RALPH: Hey, Jerry, why the hangdog look?

JERRY: Oh, I don't know. . . .

RALPH: C'mon, Jer, you're usually the happiest guy around.

JERRY: Well, you haven't been around me for some time—not since my marriage went on the rocks.

RALPH: Your marriage? Oh, gee, that's awful. You and Fran used to be so happy. What happened?

JERRY: Who knows? You know women. One day everything's fine, the next they're telling you you're

179

unfeeling, out of touch, and
generally a slob.

RALPH: So, have you split? I mean, if
I'm not intruding. . . .

JERRY: No, not yet. But Fran says if I
don't agree to counseling we're
finished!

RALPH: And you don't want to?

JERRY: You're damned straight I don't
want to. That's all bull!

Jerry doesn't know it, but the
disagreement has begun.

RALPH: Well, what do you mean by
bull?

Ralph will try to get as much
information from Jerry as he can. This
is important to prevent wasting time
and following false paths.

JERRY: [*Looks at Ralph askance.*] Hell,
what am I supposed to do? Go in
and tell some guy my problems
because my wife's unhappy?

Jerry hasn't really added anything
yet.

RALPH: Well, lots of couples in trouble
go into counseling.

JERRY: Well, I'm not "lots of couples."
Besides, Fran wants us to see this
woman therapist. Can't you just see
it? The two of them ganging up on
me, showing me it's all my fault.

Jerry didn't go for the *ad populum*
maneuver, even though it was a fair
comment.

RALPH: Hey, a good therapist doesn't
let anybody talk about blame—they
don't take sides. They focus on the
two of you communicating.

Good, Ralph is following Jerry's
lead. In a sensitive argument like this
one, you mustn't push too hard.

JERRY: Oh, yeah, "communicating"
—the word of the year.

RALPH: Well, it's really important in a
relationship, don't you think?

Now Ralph has asked a question.
Maybe he'll get somewhere.

180

JERRY: Hell, I communicate plenty. You know me, Ralph, I never shut up.

RALPH: Yeah, but I don't think yakking and communicating are exactly the same thing.

JERRY: [*Says nothing, but looks miserable.*]

Not all statements use words.

RALPH: [*Sympathetically.*] Look, if there was something wrong with your car, you'd go to a mechanic, right?

Ralph is going to try to get Jerry to see things in a different light.

JERRY: Sure.

Jerry has agreed with Ralph's hidden principle: See an expert. Now Ralph needs to test it further.

RALPH: And if you suddenly got terrible pains in your gut, you'd go to a doctor, right?

Ralph is pushing the principle.

JERRY: [*Slightly suspicious.*] Yeah, I guess so.

Jerry begins to see where this is going.

RALPH: [*Really careful now.*] And, if you started acting crazy and having nightmares or something, you might even go to a shrink, right?

JERRY: I don't know. . . .

RALPH: Of course you would, you're no fool. If something's wrong, you find an expert and get help.

Now Ralph has stated his principle and we'll see what Jerry does.

Suggesting that Jerry would be a fool to disagree is a form of *ad baculum*, but we'll let it pass.

JERRY: [*Reluctantly.*] Well, yeah, I guess so.

Jerry's agreement here is crucial.

RALPH: So, if your marriage is in trouble, you go to a marriage counselor, don't you?

> This applies the principle to Jerry's case.

JERRY: It's just so damned scary. I mean, I'm not good at exposing my so-called inner self. What if I do and Fran doesn't like what she sees?

> Note that Jerry did not actually assent to the principle. In some cases it might be important to get confirmation, but not with a subject like this.

RALPH: Hey, guy, you're right. What she's asking you to do is scary, and it's OK to be scared. But, remember what's at stake: You and Fran staying together.

> Ralph accepts Jerry's implicit agreement, and moves to a deeper level with a different argument.

JERRY: Yeah. [*Pause.*] I do love her, you know.

> Now they're talking about what's really going on.

RALPH: Then it's worth a little risk, isn't it? Hell, you might even be less of a jerk when you're finished.

> Ralph wraps up the point, and adds a joke to soften the mood.

JERRY: [*Takes a mock swing at Ralph.*] Ha! You'll always be the king of the jerks!

32

Part Three Review

QUESTIONS

Read the dialogue below and create a commentary just as I've done throughout Part Three.

1. JUDY: Mark, I really can't believe you're one of those people who thinks everyone should own a gun.

2. MARK: Do you know what would happen if the government took our guns away?

3. JUDY: Fewer people would get murdered?

4. MARK: No. *More!* Citizens would not be able to protect themselves, criminals would know that. They'd feel safe and break into every home they wanted to. Soon we'd all have to live in barred houses and be terrified to walk out at night. After that it would only be a matter of time before even daylight wasn't safe.

5. JUDY: Oh, don't be so dramatic! You've got no way of knowing if that scary story will happen.

6. MARK: I know that the right to bear arms is essential to a democracy.

7. JUDY: Then how come the first thing the U.S. Army did when it wanted to put a democracy back in Haiti was call in all the guns? Huh? Answer me that!

8. Well, the wrong people had the guns. If all the citizens had guns, then the dictator could never have stayed in power. There would have been a revolution and he'd have been thrown out.

9. You mean there would have been a bloody civil war and one of the two sides—the one with the most guns—would have won. You think everything can be solved by guns? Just go out and shoot and that's the end of it? If two kids are fighting over a toy, then one of them should get a gun and. . . .

10. Hey, just a minute! That's ridiculous and you know it. All I'm saying is that guns are blamed for a lot more things than they deserve to be.

11. Maybe, but do you really think the way to stop violence is to arm everybody? What if there were really strong penalties for carrying unregistered guns? Wouldn't that keep the criminals at bay?

12. Oh, yeah, some judge'll slap them on the hand and let them go, that's all.

13. I know, but what if they didn't? What if there were no choice? Mandatory two years with no parole for carrying an unregistered weapon?

14. I don't know. I mean they haven't. . . .

15. Yeah, but they could. If we could find a way of

controlling the criminals and have fewer guns, wouldn't that be best?

16. MARK: Sure, but target shooters still have a right to. . . .

ANSWERS

Here are my comments on this argument beginning with Statement 4. Please understand that different people may notice different things when following a dispute.

4. Mark has introduced a classic *slippery slope* fallacy. It assumes that, once the first step is taken, every further step will follow inexorably. In fact, there are many other scenarios.

5. Judy has caught the fallacy, but notice that she did not give a counter-argument, just a denial.

6. Mark is *changing the subject* so he won't have to defend his predictions.

7. Judy didn't notice, but she did use a good counter-example. If Mark's principle is that guns are "essential to democracy," why, in Haiti, did they seem to prevent it?

9. Judy is using a *straw-man* fallacy to exaggerate Mark's position.

10. Good. Mark caught the move and called Judy on it. Now, if Judy is smart, she'll notice a slight moderation in his position. This might signal an opportunity.

11. Now Judy is asking a question—that hasn't happened much in this dispute. She's offering an alternative to see if Mark might negotiate.

12. Mark responds with a *non sequitur*, a change of subject.

13. Good. Judy gets him right back to her question.

15. Mark is weakening. Judy interrupts to press home her point.

16. Mark seems to agree, but then *changes the subject*. Judy's strategy at this point should be to agree to some leeway for target-shooters, and then recap her position for Mark. At that point she'll see if he will hold to his agreement.

Appendix

Sources for More Information on Arguing Well

The best way to hone your argument skills to is argue, especially when you are in situations where not too much is at stake. This allows you to listen carefully and pay attention to what you are doing when you are not dangerously involved. You can also take advantage of situations when others are arguing and you can sit back and listen. Try to spot fallacies and mistakes; notice who is listening and who is not; identify times when the subject changes and no one notices. By doing this you are training yourself to listen and react when in a safe situation.

Many colleges and universities offer courses in argumentation. These are frequently listed under the headings "Critical Thinking" or "Informal Logic." Contact your local campus and inquire about such courses in their adult education or regular programs. These courses provide you with tools for arguing as well as partners to argue with. Do try to make sure that the instructor is qualified in the field, and not just someone assigned to the course.

There are a multitude of books containing valuable information about creative and effective ways to argue. I will only recommend a few, several at each of the various levels of expertise you might want to explore.

BASIC MATERIAL

Among popular books relating to argument, I recommend the following.

Capaldi, Nicholas. *The Art of Deception*. 2d ed. Buffalo, NY: Prometheus, 1975.

Fisher, Roger, and Ury, William. *Getting to Yes*. 2d ed. New York: Penguin, 1991.

Huff, Darrel. *How to Lie with Statistics*. New York: Norton, 1959.

INTERESTING TEXTBOOKS

If you go to your local library and search the area where books on "Critical Thinking" and "Informal Logic" are shelved, you will find many choices. Here are a few, but there are many others.

Fogelin, Robert J., and Sinnott-Armstrong, Walter. *Understanding Arguments*. San Diego: Harcourt Brace Javanovitch, 1991.

Govier, Trudy. *A Practical Study of Argument*. 2d ed. Belmont, CA: Wadsworth, 1988.

Johnson, Ralph, and Blair, J. Anthony. *Logical Self-Defense*. 3d ed. Toronto: McGraw-Hill Ryerson, 1993.

Kahane, Howard. *Logic and Contemporary Rhetoric.* 5th ed. Belmont, CA: Wadsworth, 1986.

HEAVY-DUTY READING

The field of Argumentation Theory has been changing and developing dramatically over the past 25 years. It has become multidisciplinary and draws on research, not only from philosophy, but from Communication Theory, Sociology, and Psychology as well. The following books, intended for experts in the field, are extremely dense and technical, but advanced readers might find them of interest.

Cox, J.R., and Willard, C.A. *Advances in Argumentation Theory & Research.* Carbondale, IL: Southern Illinois University Press, 1982.

Eemeren, F.H. van, Grootendorst, R., and Snoeck Henkemans, F. *Fundamentals of Argumentation Theory.* Hillsdale, NJ: Lawrence Erlbaum & Assoc., 1996.

Hall, Lavinia, ed. *Negotiation: Strategies for Mutual Gain.* Newbury Park, CA: Sage, 1983.

Johnson, Ralph, and Blair, J. Anthony, eds. *New Essays in Informal Logic.* [Available from the Department of Philosophy, University of Windsor, Windsor, Ontario N9B 3P4.]

Also in this category are the following scholarly journals: *Logic, Argumentation, Argumentation and Advocacy*, and *Philosophy & Rhetoric*

Argumentation
Editorial Office
Spuistraat 134
1012 VB Amsterdam
The Netherlands

Informal Logic
Department of Philosophy
University of Windsor
Windsor, Ontario N9B 3P4

Argumentation and Advocacy
American Forensic Association
Box 256
River Falls, WI 54022

Philosophy and Rhetoric

Pennsylvania State University Press
University Park, PA 16802

PROFESSIONAL DEVELOPMENT & SEMINARS

Through my business, Paradox Communications, 70 Withrow Avenue, Toronto, Canada M4K 1C9, I offer workshops and seminars for businesses and groups, give talks to meetings and clubs, and address social and professional functions. Depending on the needs of the client, these range from a lighthearted overview of some problems in argument to in-depth training in the techniques of argument and critical discussion.

Index

A

Advertising
  appeals in, 139–140
  and defensive arguments, 17
  and leading brands, 83
  and persuasion, 9
Appeal to force, 137–141
  appropriate situation for, 138
  basis of, 137–138
  examples of, 138–140
  nature of, 137
Argument
  building an, 29–33
  attached argument, 12–14,
    19–20
  cautions related to, 19–22
  and consistency, 39
  creative, 12, 14
  defensive, 15–16, 17
  definition of, 5–6

fallacies in. *See* Fallacies
  good versus bad, 4
  and knowledge, 51–52
  and listening, 46–49, 52
  offensive, 16–17
  situations for, 8–11
  social acceptability of, 3–5
  sources of information on,
    187–190
Argument building, 29–33
  claim, 29–30
  reasons, 31–32
  relevant difference, 39–41
Arguments, examples
  essay service as form of cheat-
    ing, 176–178
  on homosexuality, 155–158
  joining cult, 167–171
  legalization of marijuana,
    151–154

Arguments, examples *(continued)*
living together versus marriage, 164–166
marriage counseling as issue, 179–182
sex devices, sale of, 172–175
women in law enforcement, 159–163
Argumentum ad hominem. *See* Attack on the person
Argumentum ad populum. *See* Popularity fallacy
Argumentum ad verecundiam. *See* Authority fallacy
Attached argument, 12–14, 19–20
nature of, 12–14
Attack on the person, 97–106
examples of, 98, 100–103
as fallacy, 61
genetic fallacy, 105–106
responses to, 99–106
Authority fallacy, 89–96
and celebrity endorsements, 90–91
checking out experts, 94–95
and expert in appropriate field, 91–93
opinions versus facts, 93–94

B
Begging the question, fallacy of, 66–68
Black-and-white fallacy, false dilemma fallacy as, 132
Books, on argument, 188–189

C
Changing the subject, 72–81

dealing with, 76–81
examples of, 73–74, 798
refocusing opponent, 80–81
Circular reasoning, fallacy of, 64–66, 69–71
Claim, in argument, 29–30
Common practice fallacy. *See* Two wrongs fallacy
Consistency, and argument, 39
Conviction, and argument, 9, 10–11, 21
Creative argument
nature of, 12, 14
and winning argument, 24
Criminal activities, and two wrong fallacy, 136–137

D
Defeat, never admitting, 25–27
Defensive argument, nature of, 15–16, 17
Dismissal of ideas, as genetic fallacy, 106
Distortion of facts
listening for, 112
and straw-man argument, 110–112
Doubtful evidence fallacy, 119–122
and believing nothing, 120–122
checking against, 119–120
examples of, 120, 121

E
Experts, and authority fallacy, 89–96

F

Fallacies, 60–62
 appeal to force fallacy, 137–141
 attack on the person, 61,
  97–106
 authority fallacy, 89–96
 begging the question, 66–68,
  69–71
 changing the subject, 72–81
 circular reasoning, 64–66
 doubtful evidence fallacy,
  119–122
 false cause fallacy, 122–126
 false dilemma fallacy, 130–133
 genetic fallacy, 105–106
 handling in argument, 62
 hasty generalization, 126–129
 petitio principii, 64
 popularity fallacy, 83–86
 provincialism, 86
 slippery slope, 113–118
 special pleading, 37
 straw-man argument, 107–112
 two wrongs fallacy, 133–137
False cause fallacy, 122–126
 attacking false causes, 125–126
 checking against, 123–125
False dilemma fallacy, 130–133
 as black-and-white fallacy, 132
 examples of, 131–132
Family arguments, 19
Fanatics, dealing with, 36–38
Fear, and appeal to force, 137–141
Force. *See* Appeal to force

G

Genetic fallacy, 105–106
 and dismissal of ideas, 106

and origin of ideas, 105–106
Guilt, and two wrongs fallacy,
 135–137

H

Hasty generalization, 126–129
 proving generalizations wrong,
  127–129

I

Ignoratio elenchi. *See* Changing
 the subject
Intuition, 50–51

J

Journals, on argument, 189–190

K

Knowledge, and argument, 51–52

L

Listening, 46–49
 and argument, 47–49, 52
 for change of subject, 77–78
 and conversation, 47
 for distortions, 112
Losing argument
 and admitting defeat, 25–27
 and fallacies, 60–62
 reasons for, 59–60

N

Non sequitur. *See* Changing the
 subject

O

Offensive argument, nature of,
 16–17

Origin of ideas, as genetic fallacy, 105–106

P
Persuasion, in advertising, 9
Petitio principii, 64
Popularity fallacy, 83–86
  factors in popularity, 83–84
  forms of, 84–85
  handling of, 86
Principles, argument about, 42–45
Principles of argument
  Principle Principle, 42
  Principle of Rationality, 34–38
  Principle of Similar Cases, 41–45
Provincialism fallacy, 86

Q
Qualifiers, types of, 129

R
Radical positions, and straw-man argument, 108–112
Rationality, 34–38
  dealing with fanatics, 36–38
Reasons, in argument, 31–32
Relevant difference, 39–41

S
Schopenauer, Arthur, 26
Seminars, on argument, 190
Similar cases, principle of, 41–45
Skeptics, success in arguments, 122
Slippery slope, 113–118
  dealing with, 117–118
  degrees of slipperiness, 114–116
  and Principle of Similar Cases, 116
Socrates, 22
Special pleading, 37
Straw-man argument, 107–112
  and distortion of facts, 110–112
  nature of, 108–109

T
Two wrongs fallacy, 133–137
  dealing with, 135
  examples of, 133–136
  use as admission of guilt, 135–137

W
Winning argument, 23–28
  and creative argument, 24
  never admitting defeat, 25–27